You owe it to your team to read  provides a framework for mar their teams, deliver better resu of practical exercises that can be implemented straight away and are clearly drawn from extensive experience. Great for any manager who wants to improve their people management skills.

Steve Brennan, CEO, Bespoke Digital

Any manager who picks up *Mission: To Manage* will find themselves exclaiming 'that's so true!' at regular intervals. From managing teams in different locations to dealing with team members who ask too many questions (a problem I was discussing with one of my managers just this morning), the challenges Marianne presents are very real and common to managers at all levels in all industries. In typical, uncomplicated Marianne style, her solutions to these problems are simple and practical, with resources and missions to keep you on track. Her positive energy flows through the book and will leave you ready to see the potential rather than the worst in people – it's infectious and it's uplifting. Through *Mission: To Manage* Marianne shows us that leading and inspiring a team doesn't have to be mission impossible!

Kathryn Stedman, Chief Language Officer, Supertext

As business owners we all, at some point crave the Holy Grail – time freedom – to do the stuff that makes us happy. Not enough of us realise that the key to our happiness is having a happy team. A team led by an empowered and empathic managing leader. *Mission: To Manage* gives a blueprint for anyone wanting to become such a leader. An insightful read with practical tips and strategies for managers and business owners that can be implemented straight away.

Heena Thaker, Business mentor, Intentional Wealth Creation

Mission: To Manage is an essential tool for any manager who wants to be good at managing people. This book has completely refreshed my mindset, and I feel that I have rediscovered my mojo for managing my team! Thank you, Marianne, for opening my eyes to essential communication and feedback skills, and so much more!

Kelly Feltham, Practice Manager, JLA

In *Mission: To Manage* Marianne gives us a blueprint for effective people management that will help every struggling manager to become the leader their team *want* to follow!

Paul Barnes, Managing Director, MAP

Marianne encapsulates every aspect of a manager who has completed her mission. This book is a pleasure to read, it encourages the reader to reflect honestly about how they've managed in the past or what type of manager they hope to be. *Mission: To Manage* inspires the reader to view people management as a positive and enjoyable task that will bring countless benefits to the manager. Having worked with Marianne on her management and business owner courses it is no surprise that I am enthused to buy each of my managers a copy. A must read for any aspiring manager, new manager, experienced manager or business owner.

Harri Colman, Managing Director, FABRIC

This book is a must for anyone who wants to build and keep a great team motivated! It is such an easy read, with step-by-step guides to the building blocks to becoming – and continuing to develop as – a great manager and leader. It's based on sound evidence and Marianne's own experiences and values shine through in every chapter. The 'missions' at the end of each chapter push you to implement what you've learned straight away – and help dispel fears and barriers to becoming the manager your team, your business and your customers deserve!

Hilary Lloyd, Business Change and Transformation Leader

Mission:
TO MANAGE

...because managing people doesn't need to be mission impossible

FROM THE BEST-SELLING AUTHOR OF
SIMPLE LOGICAL REPEATABLE

First published in Great Britain by Practical Inspiration Publishing, 2020

ISBN   9781788601825   (print)
       9781788601818   (epub)
       9781788601801   (mobi)

Illustrations by Ben Downer

Practical Inspiration
PUBLISHING

Contents

Contents

About the author

'Marianne's McDonald's experience makes her one of the world's most qualified experts on the practicalities of implementing systems and building high performing teams.'

Marianne Page is an award-winning leader and developer of high performing teams; inspiring successful small business owners to build the simple systems and high performing team that will free them from the day-to-day of their operation; giving them back the time to enjoy a fulfilling life, confident that their business is running as it should.

Marianne developed a number of high performing teams of her own during her 27-year career as a senior manager with McDonald's, and developed over 14,000 managers and franchisees over an eight-year period as the company's Training Manager.

For the past ten years, Marianne has worked closely with successful business owners who have overcomplicated their life and their business, helping them to develop the systems and the structure that will make their operation consistent, and free them to work on their business rather than in it. During this time she has also worked with the managers of these businesses, individuals who have often been thrust into a management position without any of the necessary training. Through her Managers' Development Programme, Marianne has supported and developed these managers, developing the skills, strategies and confidence they need to be successful in their role.

Marianne is the bestselling author of *Simple Logical Repeatable*, *The McFreedom Report* and *Process to Profit*, and can be contacted via the usual social media channels or via the Marianne Page Limited website – www.mariannepage.co.uk

Foreword

No successful business ever became successful without great managers.

Great managers don't just make sure that stuff gets done, they galvanise teams of people to *want* to deliver – for themselves, their managers and their business.

For any employee, their manager is one of the most thought-about people in their lives. They go into work thinking about them, work with them through the day and come home from work talking about them to their family and friends.

Being a manager is a big responsibility and it can feel very daunting to anyone new to it or struggling to get results. But it can also be incredibly rewarding.

Through working with Marianne and following her framework, I have watched the managers in our business flourish into respected leaders. They have developed from being good technicians with limited output to multi-faceted managers who can lead a team to multiply their output.

Marianne is the real deal when it comes to navigating the complex world of people management. She is renowned for helping businesses to systemise, but from her time at McDonald's she recognises that systems only exist to make people's lives easier. You need good people to work the systems and good managers to get the best out of their people.

Her experience is second to none and in *Mission: To Manage*, she provides a practical framework for developing inexperienced and struggling managers into mature and resilient professionals.

Mission: To Manage will allow the managers in your company to self-identify their preferred management style and to become the very best version of themselves.

Paul Barnes, Managing Director, MAP

What to expect from
Mission: To Manage

*M*ission: *To Manage* is your blueprint for becoming the leader-manager your team members want to follow. The book is divided into seven chapters which each deal with one of the seven essential management skills you need to master in order to achieve your goal.

1. Your mindset
2. Your team-building skills
3. Your team's performance
4. Your feedback skills
5. Your communication skills
6. Your team's rhythm
7. Your personal management system

To accompany each chapter you will have access to worksheets and templates that you can download (via links in the Resources section at the back of the book) and work through, either on your own or, where appropriate, with your team.

At the end of each chapter and after key sections, you will be challenged to complete a Mission related to what you've just learned. Each Mission will make you stop and think, and then take action. This book is all about action and implementation. There is no point in reading any business or self-help book if you're not going to do anything with what you learn.

What I recommend you do is read through the whole book once, and then go back through it, chapter by chapter in whatever order makes most sense to you, completing the Missions I've set you – making both the behavioural and operational changes that will build your skills and help you to build your high-performing team.

Your determination and persistence in mastering the seven management essentials in the chapters that follow will determine your success as a manager.

Enjoy the process. Have fun with it. You are a great leader-manager in the making!

Good luck!

Prologue

People management: Is it really mission impossible?

No, of course not. Anyone with the right values, the right mindset and the right development can become a good manager.

Just like every other role you've ever learned, it is a series of skills and strategies that can be learned, applied and built upon, day-to-day, month-to-month and year-to-year. As long as you're prepared to work at it, and accept that you'll always be learning, you can be a *really* good manager.

It doesn't matter how old you are, how many letters you have after your name (the fewer the better in my experience), how you were brought up or what personality you have – your starting point does not determine how successful you'll be.

Leader or manager?

Back in the day, there was a very clear distinction between a leader and a manager. In a nutshell, leaders were considered to do all of the strategy and big-picture thinking, while managers did all the organising of resources and looked after execution of the strategy. In the corporate world, this can often still be the case, but in the world of the successful small business there is a very real need for leaders to be managers and vice versa.

Which raises the age-old question about whether leaders are born or made.

As I said back when I wrote my first book *Process to Profit*, I believe that without doubt, some people are born leaders; they have a charisma and an energy about them that can't be taught or learned. Some come from backgrounds where there were no positive role models and yet they still emerged to inspire and lead others.

Equally though, I know that you can learn leadership behaviours. You can learn to respect others, to be consistent, fair, direct and so on. And it's fair to say that charisma on its own, without the leadership behaviours to match it, can be a dangerous thing. Remember Bill Clinton? He is a great example of a man with amazing charisma and energy, who was a little flawed when it came to being a leader.

Every manager needs to be a leader and every leader needs to be a manager. In your role as a leader you'll make sure that your team feel comfortable, that they grow as people and contribute to achieving team goals. But people need structure to succeed, and as a manager you need the skills to organise your team's activity and make best use of the resources you have to deliver on your goals.

A manager without leadership skills won't optimise their team's potential. On the other hand, a leader without management skills will be chaotic and drive their team mad.

Keep this in mind as you work through this book…

Great leaders are also managers because they understand the best way to get the work done to achieve their goals.

Great managers are also leaders because they know how to make best use of their own skills and talent and more importantly how to get the best out of every individual in their team to deliver even greater results.

> *Before you are a leader, success is all about growing yourself. When you become a leader, success is all about growing others.*
>
> Jack Welch – American business executive

Who are you and how did you get here?

I guess this question can be read in two ways:

1. How did you become a people manager? How did you get to the position you're in?
2. What brought you to this book? What are you struggling with or need help with?

Maybe you're a business owner – you started your own business and with success came the need for a small team, that you now feel unqualified to manage. You're doing ok, but you know you can do better.

Or perhaps you were promoted from within the team – the business you work in has grown and your boss needs help in managing the growing team. You were really good at your old job, and you've been in the business a long time too, so you were the natural choice for manager – but you're struggling to find your feet in your new job.

Of course, you could have been hired as a manager. Maybe you've been a manager in another business, or perhaps you did a management degree, and this is your first job – either way, you recognise that you still have a lot to learn to put the theory into practice and get the best out of your new team.

However you got here, you will know more about management than you probably realise. You'll have been 'managed' by teachers at school, by the manager where you had your first part-time job, by the captain of your sports team – maybe you were the captain yourself! So I'm sure that you've experienced good and bad leadership; individuals that you would follow into a burning building, and individuals that you would push into one!

And the truth is, we learn from both. I know I did.

At one stage I worked for a woman who was very black and white, who wanted everyone in her team to be the same, who never looked at the individual and the skills they brought to the team, but wanted them to be mini versions of herself. She was all about command and control, a micro-manager who used her position of power to bully people into doing things her way.

Happily, for me she was a one-off, a great example of how I was not going to manage my teams going forward, and I had plenty of great leaders around me to model. Others are not so lucky, and 'grow up' believing that being a manager is all about power and authority, about throwing your weight around. All too often, as in life generally, the bullied become the bully.

Management stereotypes

There are a few manager stereotypes – you might recognise a couple from your own experience.

The budgie (everyone's best friend)
This manager wants to be one of the team. They hate confrontation and giving constructive feedback and would rather ignore poor standards than confront an individual, no matter the consequences. They often work late to help out or to correct mistakes the team have made. They still know all the gossip, revelling in their role as agony aunt. Ultimately, they want to be everyone's best friend first and their manager second.

The woodpecker (micro-manager)
This manager is obsessed with the details – everything has to be perfect and 'just so'. Mistakes get on their nerves because their team should be able to get it right by now. They want reports at every stage of a project, and will regularly check up on the team to see what they're doing and that it's being done exactly as they would do it.

The peacock (aloof/hands-off manager)
This manager operates from a distance. They give minimal information to the team about what they want and then leave them to get on with it. If things go well they take the

credit, if things go badly they blame the team. They're rarely around for advice or support. Always out of the office or in meetings with the boss. They don't get involved in the day-to-day because they don't see it as their job – they have people to deal with all that.

The seagull (non-stick manager)

This is the manager who swoops in, dumps all over everyone and then flies off again. They are erratic, poorly prepared and extremely arrogant. They damage team morale by treating them like idiots, talking down to them and blaming everyone else for their failures. When things turn out badly or they run into a problem, they swoop in to assign blame and then become the hero by sorting it out.

The eagle (inspirational leader)

This is the well-respected manager that the team would walk through fire for. They're inspirational, firm but fair and hands-on when they're needed. They do what they say they'll do and are always straight with their team, who know exactly where they stand. They give credit whenever possible, and when there's a problem, they take responsibility. Always looking to develop their team and better their leadership skills, they have a great relationship with their boss.

They are the leader-manager we all aspire to be every day.

Which are you?

Do you recognise yourself in any of these? Maybe you're a mixture of a few because you haven't yet worked out your own style. Maybe you're trying too hard to be the manager you think you should be – the woodpecker or the peacock maybe – when just being yourself and being true to your own values might lead you down the path to becoming an eagle.

Model the best

What I mean by modelling is looking for behaviours and characteristics that you admire in others, and making them your own. Think of how children copy their parents – talking like them, acting like them, making the same gestures and so on. The same happens at work. Usually unconsciously, we adopt mannerisms, phrases and behaviours of the people we hang round with a lot.

What I'm asking you to do here is become conscious of that 'copying' and choose to model the best behaviours of those around you, and stop modelling the behaviours that don't fit you or your values. This isn't about you becoming someone you're not or changing your personality, it's about spotting a behaviour that you admire or respect in someone else, and building it into how you behave.

When I think of leaders who are loved and/or respected, I think of Nelson Mandela, Mahatma Gandhi, Pope Francis, Malala Yousafzai. For me – and I know it's my personal opinion – they all share a number of values, which are demonstrated in their behaviours:

- They care.
- They have a sense of responsibility for their people/ the people who follow them.

- They set a good example.
- They believe passionately in what they are doing, and don't waiver from it.
- They inspire others.
- They put the well-being of others before self-interest.
- They are believable, straightforward, honest people who you could imagine yourself sitting down to dinner with, having a good conversation with, having them listen to you and be interested in you.

Learn from the worst

On the other hand, when I think of leaders I don't respect, the likes of Saddam Hussein, Kim Jong-un, Winnie Mandela and Hitler spring to mind. People with values very different to my own. People who share a number of characteristics and behaviours that I want to avoid at all costs:

- They are self-obsessed.
- They are arrogant, bordering on narcissistic.
- They are greedy.
- They inspire fear and/or division.
- They are bullies and autocrats.
- They want what's best for them and don't care about anyone else.
- They abuse their position of power.

Take time to reflect on these lists, and think about which list your team would put you on. Hopefully on the first, but what about on your bad days?

Recognising your strengths and your failings now will have a big impact on what you get from the rest of this book.

Look around you. Think about the people in your life who you respect and admire. What is it about them that makes you feel this way? What is it they do? What is it they don't do? What behaviours could you learn from and build into your own behaviours day-to-day to make you a better person, a better manager, a better leader?

What is a manager?

The four roles of a manager

Now you know your good role models from your bad, it's time to learn the other roles you need to fill to become the leader-manager that your team admire, respect and want to follow.

1. Leader–manager
We've already talked about the fact that these days, you can't be one without the other – you have to have the skills of both a leader and a manager. Way back in the Industrial Revolution, managers were solely the coordinators of resources, micro-managing the workforce to make sure that they did what they were meant to while they were in the factory, mill or wherever.

Occasionally their role might tip over into coaching, but it would be quite rare.

Here in the 2020s it's not enough to just tell your employees what to do. Today's generation are not the 'tell me how high you want me to jump' people of days gone by. They want to know why they're jumping, and why this high?

'Why do you want things done this way? How is it going to help me? How is it going to make my life easier? How is it going to help the business?'

So as leader-manager you need to think through the answers to these questions before they're asked, and communicate them clearly to involve and engage your team in every way you can, to motivate and inspire your team through your example and your respect for each of them as individuals.

I've never bought into this idea that you have to be born a leader – that you can't become one.

I do agree that there are natural leaders who were born to lead, but I also believe that leadership is a skill that can be developed. The context of your surroundings, a particular situation or the people you have with you can also bring out the leader that no one knew existed.

- You can learn the behaviours of a leader.
- You can learn to think like a leader.
- You can learn to communicate like a leader.
- You can become a leader.
- Your team needs a leader.

2. Manager–coordinator

In this role you look after the nuts and bolts of the job, getting the operation to work as it should, using the business resources effectively and efficiently. In this role, you're running your training system, preparing rotas, following up on the equipment maintenance, keeping the day-to-day of the operation flowing without a hitch. It's a vital part of your role.

3. Manager–coach

One of the best football managers ever was Sir Alex Ferguson. From the outside he was viewed as ruthless – a very hard-hitting, overly demanding manager – but he always got the best out of every individual. He didn't always have the most talented individuals in his teams, but with very few exceptions, everyone who worked with him fulfilled their true potential.

He knew when to put an arm around somebody and when to give one of the team a proverbial kick up the bum. That was his role as a coach, getting the very best out of people, teaching every employee the values of the organisation – in his case, the football club – making sure every one of them knew that 'this is how we do things around here, this is our culture, this is how we operate, these are the standards we expect'.

Coaching your team – giving them the skills they need to do their job well and developing them as people – is going to play a major role in gaining their respect for you as their manager. Which brings me nicely onto your fourth and often forgotten role.

4. Manager-mentor

It was a mentor I really respect who said to me: 'From day one, train the employee and develop the individual.' Take the new employee and train them to follow your systems. Give them all of the skills they need to do the job to the highest standard. At the same time, develop the individual to help them to grow as a person – to fulfil their potential – to be the best they can be.

Your role as a mentor is not about teaching them the skills and the tactics of the business – that's your coaching job. As a mentor it's all about helping the individual to become a more rounded person, a great team member, maybe even a leader themselves.

If you work with young people, you may be working with someone who's having their first experience in a job and may have no idea how to behave in the work environment. In my first role as a manager in McDonald's, I had to deal with a lot of 16–18 year-olds – often youngsters who wouldn't tidy their room at home, or do the dishes, or cooperate with their siblings.

My first job was to help them to understand the business values – the importance of doing things right first time, of working as part of a team, of continuous learning. I would often take my new starter to one side and have a quiet word with them if they were behaving in a way that didn't fit our culture or was having an effect on the rest of the team – things that are really important for them to get right if they want to get on – whether that's in your business, or someone else's.

Sharing your life experience (however young you are) and the lessons that you've learned that have helped to shape you, with someone who's just getting started or who's struggling, is a hugely important part of your role as a manager.

So you need to be a leader, a coordinator, a coach and a mentor. We're not asking much from you here!

The role of a manager is constantly evolving

In the past you could demand respect, now you have to earn it from your people, from your team. And if you don't... they'll simply move on.

In the past it was expected that as a manager you would show no emotion, no sign of weakness. Even when you knew you were wrong, you would act as if you knew that you were right. Now it's important to embrace your own vulnerability, to embrace the fact that you are human and can make mistakes; to be able to say, 'sorry I got that wrong'.

You don't lose respect when you're vulnerable, you gain it.

In the past, as a manager, you would be supported by your employees, who would work for you. These days the most successful leader-managers work *with* their team, using the language of 'we' versus 'me and them'. *We* all work together to achieve one clear goal.

Management frustrations

The role of a manager has changed, and continues to change and evolve, but there are a few frustrations that many managers can't seem to overcome.

Frustration #1

How to get people to do what you say, without having to micro-manage them, to cajole them or threaten them with discipline. How to get them to do what you say, to the standard that you want, every time.

Frustration #2

How to give feedback without it turning into confrontation; without making someone cry or have any sort of emotional reaction.

How does that work? How can you give somebody feedback, that leaves them thinking, 'Ok, I'm going to get that right next time' rather than 'I hate my manager!'? How do you avoid giving feedback that leaves them feeling deflated or angry when what you really wanted was to inspire and motivate them to improve their performance?

Frustration #3

How to manage the team, please the boss and get your own work done too.

When you're promoted into a management role you're very often expected to do the job that you always did in addition to managing people. Like you suddenly turn into a superhero, able to turn an eight-hour working day into a 16-hour working day! Oh wait... that *is* what you do!

How do you manage that?

Because you definitely don't want to be doing all of your work and all of your team's work.

You don't want to be the manager that nobody listens to and you don't want to let your boss down. You want to continue to be an asset to the business.

You want to continue to progress, develop and improve, and hopefully rise further in the business.

Through the pages of this book you have the opportunity to learn what it takes to overcome these three frustrations – to develop the skills and understand the strategies that you need to be the leader your team will follow, respected and trusted by everyone you work with, without burning out.

Your mission

Take time to reflect on what you've read in this section. Ask yourself:

- Where do I sit in all of this?
- What am I good at? Am I good at coordinating or coaching?
- Do I lead or do I command?

- Are there individuals in my team who could do with a little mentoring?
- What action am I going to take as a result of what I've learned about myself?

Chapter 1

Mastering your mindset

Being a great leader begins in your mind.

Power vs responsibility

How you show up as a leader depends on what you truly believe is the answer to the question, is management power or is it responsibility?

There are plenty of managers, new and old, who see their position as one of power, who believe in command and control, who revel in the opportunity to treat people as their serfs. But for me, with the step up to manager comes a big responsibility.

As a manager you are responsible for getting the very best out of the individuals you've been asked to lead and manage; to help those individuals to fulfil their potential and to mould them into a team that delivers results for the business.

How you handle that responsibility – how you embrace the challenge (because that's what it is) of managing your team, how willing you are to learn how to do it well and keep learning every day – is going to dictate how well-respected you are, how well your team works with you and how much you achieve together.

Decide right now – are you going to be a 'Go' or a 'Let's go' manager? A 'lead from the front' manager or a micro-manager with a big stick?

What you believe in matters

How you *live* what you believe in matters even more, because leadership is action not position. It's what you do that counts, not what you say you'll do.

I'm sure you've heard the term 'values'. People talk about values a lot without really understanding what they are and why they're important. There may be a list of your business values up on the wall where you work – maybe they were well thought through, maybe they were downloaded from the internet. But what are they really all about?

The word value comes originally from the Latin word *valere*, which means *force*. In old French it then became *valoir*, which means *to be worth*, before becoming our English word *values*, which we define as *principles or standards of behaviour; your individual and personal judgement of what is important in life.*

Your values are a central part of who you are: who you want to be as a person, as a leader and as a manager; the lines you won't cross in the way you operate; the way you want to be with friends, family and colleagues.

Your values are your internal compass. They guide every decision, every behaviour and every action that you take.

When you go against your values, you feel it in your gut. Your gut tells you that what you've done isn't right – you feel physically uncomfortable – whereas when you're in line with your values, everything feels just right.

What are your values?

Whenever I ask this question in a group setting – a workshop, a networking event – the same two words are always trotted out: 'honesty' and 'integrity'. And yes, of course, you want to be honest, always, and yes, absolutely, you want to demonstrate integrity. But for me these are the most basic of values – the foundations of being a decent human being.

When I'm talking about values, I'm talking about the things that make you, you. The things that your family, friends and team would say really matter to you. The things that make you angry, the things that delight you, the things that you rail passionately for or against.

They are the force that drives you; the things that show your worth; the heart and soul of who you are.

Maybe it's your attention to detail. Maybe it's that you always tell it like it is. Maybe it's that you listen in order to understand.

An architect client of mine was struggling to define what his values were. He'd trotted out honesty and integrity and then got stuck. I'd noticed though that in conversation over the two days I'd spent with him, he'd said a number of times that he believed that there was always another way, another viewpoint. He told me that every time his architects were going to look at a new project, he would say to them: 'Whatever your first thoughts are, remember, there's always another way, so look for it. Look for all the options. Broaden your view.'

It was something he believed in strongly, something he lived by, a force that drove him to look at other viewpoints, other options; to expand his thinking.

It was clearly one of his values.

So what are yours?

Your mission

Download the Values worksheet (see Resources section at the back of the book) and ask yourself 'what are my values and how do they show themselves day-to-day?' Ask the people closest to you, who know you best. Ask your team who work with you every day. What is it that you *show* you value – that you live by?

Please don't go down the cliché route – picking a bunch of things that sound good, putting them on a poster and sticking them on a wall. I've seen that so many times, and nobody is fooled by it. When what is up on the wall is not played out day-to-day in the business, or in your team, it's a waste of paper and ink.

Values lead to culture

The culture of your team will be built around *your* values. Whatever you *show* is important, whatever you measure, whatever you follow up on will be what your team focus on, will become the things that are important to them too, and ultimately will become the culture of your team.

It's easy to recognise the symptoms of poor culture:

- Lots of sickness and no-shows
- Sloppy work – lots of mistakes and things missed
- No communication – and poor communication, most of it on email
- No respect for each other or the manager
- Clock-watching

So what can you do to change a poor culture if you have one, or to create a positive culture if you're just starting to build your team?

As a manager, the first place you need to look is in the mirror. Look at the way you behave, what you follow up on, what you praise, how you communicate with individuals, what you *show* the team is important to you every single day.

If you say that keeping commitments is important to you, do you always turn up to every meeting on time?

If you say you're going to have a one-to-one with a team member, do you ever cancel it because you're just too busy, or something *more important* has come up?

If you say that feedback is important for personal growth, do you listen to and reflect on feedback from your team?

Shadow of the leader

Whether we like it or not, as managers we cast a shadow over the people in our team, and just like a child will mimic (or model) their parents, our team will mimic our behaviours and actions, follow our cues, develop our traits. It's important that you understand the power of your shadow, and model the behaviours that you want to see in your team, because your example will be followed.

Your values come first, your team culture follows.

Take a blank sheet of paper and draw a picture of yourself – it doesn't have to be a great piece of art, a stickman or a rough outline will do.

Then on the right of your picture, write down all of the things that represent you on a good day.

- What are you like when you're at your best?
- How do you act?
- What do you say? Or not say?
- How are you with the team?
- What's your energy like?

Then, on the left of your picture, write down all of the things that represent you on a bad day.

Spend at least 15 minutes reflecting on the shadow you cast over the team. Develop at least one strategy for eliminating, or at least minimising your 'bad' days.

Harness the power of your big MAC

As you've probably gathered over the course of this chapter, mastering your mindset on its own is not enough. Your positive *mindset* has to be backed up by positive *action* and *consistency* – your own personal big MAC.

Check your mindset

I had a 'conversation' with a guy on LinkedIn some time ago, who was telling anyone who would listen that we need to accept that employees are all lazy – they'll do the minimum possible to get by; that they are stupid – they can't even follow the most basic of instructions and need to be micro-managed to within an inch of their lives; and that they are devious – they're out to get you, to undermine you, to sabotage your work. He argued that if we all accepted that, we'd have much better lives because we'd walk into being a manager with our eyes wide open.

What a depressing viewpoint! I pity him, and anyone unfortunate to work for him.

Naturally, I have a very different point of view! I believe that people are full of potential. They are smart and caring and fun. If you show you care about them as a person, they will try hard for you; if you believe in them and show them that you do, they will start to believe in themselves and you'll be amazed by what you get back.

What are *your* beliefs about people? Have you picked up on the negativity of other managers, or are you excited about what's possible for the individuals in your team?

Of course, I recognise that there are exceptions to my positive picture. There are individuals who are just not right for you and your team – but they *will* be right somewhere else, doing something that's perfect for them and their skills.

Everybody has potential.

Let me tell you a story to illustrate my point.

Anna's story

This is a true story, but with the names and situation changed to protect the person it relates to.

Anna worked in my office. She'd been hired to work in the office restaurant, and she'd always been difficult – a belligerent and moody employee, rude to the people she was serving and happy to stand round chatting while people waited at the tills. It was a bit of a shock to many people when she was moved into the team who ran the switchboard and reception, instead of being moved out the front door. Perhaps upsetting the odd important visitor was considered less of a danger than upsetting the office employees on a daily basis.

A year or so after her move, I was promoted into a position that made me Anna's boss and I immediately began to take the necessary steps to manage her performance. In doing this, I began to learn things about her that I hadn't known before:

- She had come from a very poor background.
- She'd left school with no qualifications.
- She was the sole provider for her three children, and it was clear that she was a very loyal mother to them.

I also learned that she loved working for McDonald's, that McDonald's had been the first organisation to give her a chance and crucially, that she had never really had any feedback from previous managers about her behaviour.

It made me think twice about the road I was taking her down, and pushed me to ask myself what I could do better; what options I had to unleash her potential and get the best out of her.

So I moved her into the post room – out of the firing line of visitors and most staff, and into a role where she could show-case her organisational skills – I figured that as a mother of three with a full-time job, she clearly had them!

Oh my life! What a change!

Not quite overnight, but over time she made the post room her domain and began to really enjoy her job, taking owner-ship for the role and setting the standard for the two juniors who worked with her to follow.

The post was never late – she went out of her way to get important letters out, even if it meant running to the post office herself – and if someone was waiting for an important delivery to arrive, she would stay at her station, sometimes for up to three hours after her shift – no overtime, no special reward, just her own professional standards and determination that nothing would be missed on her watch.

It was a real joy to watch her in action, and a constant reminder to me of what's possible when you look for the spark inside someone, that will light them up.

That's what I want for you!

I want you to feel the joy that comes from taking people who lack confidence, or who challenge you, or who are maybe just new to a role at whatever age, and helping them to become the best version of themselves, helping them to fulfil their potential. It really is a joy for me, and I want you to feel some of that joy.

I want you to move away from the dark side – associating employees with HR, legal, trouble, stress – and move into the light, and the fun of building a high performing, highly engaged team.

Take positive action every day

I like to watch films, and one of my favourites is *Gladiator* which tells the story of a Roman general, Maximus Decimus Meridius, who has close ties with the Roman emperor, Marcus Aurelius. When the emperor's son Commodus strangles his ageing father and names himself the new emperor, he figures that one of his main opponents will be Maximus, his father's favourite. So he tries to have Maximus executed, but the plan goes sour when Maximus escapes from his executioners, is sold into slavery and made into a gladiator.

Maximus loses everything – his titles, his army, his estate and his family. He is made into a slave, the lowest member of the Roman Empire. He loses his independence and his life, becoming the property of his master who sends him daily into the arena to kill or be killed in front of thousands of spectators.

The film shows how – through the force of his will, through his desire for a just revenge for the murder of his wife and child and most importantly, through his goodness and the decency of his values – Maximus succeeds in winning the hearts of the Roman mob, and defeating Commodus, the evil emperor.

The film teaches us a crucial lesson about the power of an individual's values, because it's not through his skill as a gladiator or as a warrior, or his skill with his sword that Maximus defeats evil, but with his mind and his heart. He has courage, resilience and a singular belief in the power of good to triumph over evil.

But what has that got to do with taking positive action, I hear you ask?

Well, there's a particular line in the film that has stuck with me since I first saw it years ago: 'What we do in life echoes in eternity.'

A line that is so powerful because it's so true.

What we do today – what we say and what we do – creates our future.

You are creating your future, right now, through the action you are taking. The fact that you're reading this book (regardless of how good or otherwise you rate it) will help to shape what happens next for you, both as a manager and as a person.

Just think about that for a second. The actions that you take today are going to shape your future.

So…

- If you want to build a high performing team, what are you going to do today to move one step closer to it?

- If you want to turn round a troublesome employee, what are you going to do today to start building a better relationship with that person?
- If you want to have more influence with your boss, what are you going to do today to show them that you understand what they need from you?

What we do today creates our future. Take positive action every day.

Be consistent

The final element of your big MAC is consistency – something that every team is looking for from their manager, and every manager is looking for from their team.

Remember your shadow of the leader – if you want consistency, then you need to be consistent.

Consistent with your energy

You'll know people yourself who have great energy, they're passionate, they're positive, they're enthusiastic and they lift everyone else's energy often just by walking through the door. As managers, these people encourage and motivate the whole team, individual by individual. If someone makes a mistake they'll deal with it quietly and take responsibility with the boss; if someone's done a great job, they'll praise them loudly and make sure they get the credit for their work. Be *that* person. Consistently.

Consistent in keeping your commitments
Do what you say you're going to do. Respect other people and their time, as well as your own.

Consistent in developing your team
Give your team the training and the tools they need to take full ownership for their role, then trust them to get on with it, creating a culture of ownership and accountability.

Consistent in giving feedback
Give honest and constructive feedback. Always. And regularly.

Consistent in being firm but fair
Lead with your head and your heart. Understand that everything in life is not black and white and remember that it's possible to show empathy without lowering your standards. Sit people down and have a really honest chat. What's going on here? What can I do to help you to improve?

Look at things from a position of responsibility rather than power. What am *I* doing or not doing that's causing this? What am *I* saying that's having this effect? When you think about what *you* could do to improve a situation or improve the performance of an individual within your team, you're leading with your head and your heart.

Consistent in showing your passion for the business culture
Managers gain respect when they are completely bought into the vision and values of the business. They talk about the business as if it's their name above the door. They're

consistently looking to help the business progress and have a contagious enthusiasm for achieving results.

Consistent in making decisions

Don't be wishy washy. Understand the values of the business, understand your goals and priorities, and make decisions based on solid information and facts. You may make mistakes, you may make the wrong decision, but being willing to make a decision consistently will earn you respect.

Respect as a manager is hard to win and very easy to lose, but armed with the right leader-manager mindset, with your true values lived through your actions every day, and with consistency in how you show up, you can begin to earn it from your team.

Your mission

What actions are you going to take that will move you towards the future that you want for yourself, as a manager, as a parent, as a friend, as an employee? Take time to think about this and then commit to one action that you're going to take today in your role as a manager, and one that you will take in your role as a parent, friend or family member.

Chapter 2

Mastering your team-building skills

Not every group of people working together is a team.

Building a team is not a 'done once and it's done' sort of activity. Ask any coach or manager of a sports team and they'll tell you that building a team is something that you have to work at every day. It's both an art and a science, and the manager who can consistently build and maintain a high performing team is worth their weight in gold to both their boss and the business.

Whether you're building your team from scratch, or you've taken over a team that you're still getting to know, there are key skills and strategies you need to master to get it right, and keep getting it right.

Building your team from scratch

Not many managers get the opportunity to build a team from the ground up – to have that blank canvas to work on – to have the chance to select and develop the right people first time. I had that opportunity once during my career with McDonald's, and it was fun! Cherry-picking people who shared my values and had the variety of skills I needed in the team; developing the systems for us all to follow; building the individuals into a team that rocked... if I say so myself!

Your relationship with any new team member begins before you even meet them. It begins with you working out who you need – what role you want to fill, the sort of person you're looking for, what skills and values they must have to fit both the role and the team. This person then needs to be uncovered, nurtured and developed, just like any personal relationship you've ever had. In fact, there are so many similarities between the two, let's look at your employee journey in those terms.

Awareness and attraction

First, you let your ideal partners know that you're available – maybe you tell your friends and family that you're looking for love, or maybe you start going to places where you know your ideal partner may hang out, or, more likely these days, you put your profile up on a dating site, sharing the things about yourself that you hope will attract the right person to you.

How you write this profile is so important. You can't afford to be too modest, to understate the things that make you special, that make you, you. But equally you can't tell lies; you can't over-exaggerate or pretend you're something or someone you're not.

Writing a job advert for a team member is just like writing your profile for a dating site. If you want to attract the right person for you, it's vital that you showcase who you *really* are, and why the *right* person will love you. You want that right person to be reading your profile, going 'Oh yes, finally – someone who sounds just perfect for me; who loves the things I love, shares the same whacky sense of humour, has the same values. This one's for me!'

How to write an attractive job ad

How many job ads have you seen that are inspiring, make the job sound great, make the business sound like a fun place to work? Not many, I bet. Too many businesses allow the recruitment site to dictate how they present their ad, and too many managers allow their boss to pull together the ad and to manage the hiring process alone and have no involvement in hiring this person who needs to be a good fit for *their* team.

Just like your dating profile, your job ad needs to show off your business and the role you want to fill, in the best light, yet so many are dull, state the facts in uninspiring language and attract way too many people who would never be right for your business or your team.

For me, a job ad should be made up of three parts:

1. Purpose of the business
'Our business is focused on…' This is where you share your business vision; where you talk about what you are looking to achieve, what you want to do for your clients, how you want to help them.

Build the picture of your team – how your team are all focused on what's best for the customer, that you work hard and play hard – that sort of thing.

You're looking to get them excited about the prospect of working with you.

2. Purpose of the role

'This role is crucial to our success' is a great line to start this section with.

How does this role fit into your business? How does it make things easier or better for the rest of the team or for your customers?

Why is it important that the 'right' person has this role?

Even if it is a relatively minor role in the business, it must be important or you wouldn't be hiring – so share how important it is to you and the business here.

3. Pen portrait

This section is as unusual as it's important – you won't see many pen portraits in your competitors' job ads – but for your ideal candidate it's gold dust. Always written in 'their' words, your pen portrait highlights the values that your new employee will share with you and gives them a feel not only for what they'll be doing and how they'll be doing it, but also crucially, how they'll be feeling! It builds such a clear picture for them that they'll read it and, if they are a good fit, they'll be able to say 'that's me!'

Your job ad is all about attraction, so at this stage no detail and no big list of what the ideal candidate must be able to do.

How to write an attractive job description

Your job description will be attached to your job ad to give your candidate a little more info about the role, but it shouldn't be an exhaustive list of everything that you want the person to do or what they'll be 'responsible for'.

You want your job description to be clear and to the point. You want it to be focused on the right things, on the really important aspects of what the role will deliver for the business, not on absolutely every single detail, every single task that you want this person to do when they come into the job.

You'll hear a lot of managers say: 'Oh yeah, but I don't want anybody turning around and saying, "I'm not doing that, it's not on my job description". Well no, you don't, and if you're really worried about that, you can add a cover-all phrase to your job description that says '... and anything else that we think is necessary to your role'.

But to be honest, in the sort of team that I want to help you create – where you're hiring people who share your values – you're not going to have the sort of person who'll only do something if it's in their job description. And equally, you're not going to be the sort of manager who holds someone to the letter of their job description when you begin to develop them.

Here's an example of the full job description:

JOB DESCRIPTION	DATE
Operations Manager	24-4-20

PURPOSE OF THE BUSINESS

To help business owners like you to have a business that supports your life rather than one that runs it, by taking the resentment and fear out of systemising your business; making it easy, fun, and simply 'the way we do things round here'.

PURPOSE OF THE ROLE

This role is crucial to our success. Our Operations Manager will ensure that we do what we say we will; that we keep our commitments to each other and to our clients; someone who will pay attention to the detail, someone who frees up our CEO to fulfil her role as visionary and creator, giving her time to focus on the needs of our clients and the growth of our business. Our Operations Manager is the oil in the machine, making sure everyone has the resources they need to do their job to the high standards that we expect.

REPORTING MANAGER

RESPONSIBLE FOR

• Keeping our planning cycle on track

• Team performance

• Operational systems, complete with How To Guides

• Campaign management

• Event management

• Financial administration

ESSENTIALS FOR THE ROLE

• Attention to detail

• Rapport building skills

• Sense of humour

• Great at communication across different levels

• Ability to simplify the complex

• Self confidence

• Excellent organisational skills

• Ability to work under pressure

KEY ACCOUNTABILITIES

General Management
- Delivery of 90 day goals including follow-up with other team members
- Team and individual performance
- Weekly team meetings
- Development of one right way to do everything in the business
- Day to day management of our operation

Marketing
- Delivery of the marketing plan
- Liaison with JV partners to set up and manage events
- Manage the FB Live system
- Gather video testimonials from existing clients
- Ensure the smooth-running of all campaigns

Products
- Ensure there is always a good stock of Marianne's books, and send out as required
- Manage the branding of all programmes
- Manage printing of brochures and programme workbooks

Finance
- Prepare monthly reports for MP in liaison with book-keeper
- Deliver revenue and profit targets
- Manage cash flow

PEN PORTRAIT

I relish a challenge and love the opportunity to take something that's disorganised and a bit hit or miss and turn it into something that's streamlined and consistent. I see myself as the oil in the machine, making everything work as it should – smoothly, with as little friction as possible. I really enjoy planning and working out logistics too, making sure that something like an event runs to budget and without a hitch. I take great pride in that – nothing gets missed, or forgotten on my watch. I love leading a team and getting the best out of each individual. I also really enjoy working as a team member and staying one step ahead of those who rely on me – I always have their back.

The most effective job descriptions are focused on outcomes and results – not what you want the person *to be responsible for*, but what you want them *to achieve* – a clear picture of what they will deliver for your team, and for the business.

Remember, we're still in the attraction phase here.

We're still looking to stand out from the crowd.

We want to get our ideal candidate excited about the prospect of finding their ideal place to work.

We want to be as attractive as possible.

The first interaction – invite to interview

As with any online dating, the first interaction with your ideal candidate may well be an exchange of emails. What sort of first impression are you going to make? Is your communication going to be slow, sloppy and short, or will you reply quickly, professionally and in a style that showcases your personality?

Too many businesses show little respect for the people who have taken time to apply for a job with them. Most don't even get the courtesy of a reply to say 'Thanks, but no thanks', let alone any feedback about why you didn't feel they were right for your job. A lack of time is always the excuse that's trotted out, but think for a second what it says about your values to be willing to leave someone hanging, not knowing whether they're being considered or not. What sort of a reputation might you and your business start to get?

It may be a cliché, but you're really not going to get a second chance to make a great first impression.

The first date – the interview

So, we're at the point now where you think you've found someone who might be right for you – it's time for the first date. In team-building terms, we're talking about the interview.

How are you going to prepare for it?

What do you want to get out of it?

What would the answers to these questions be if this was a first date?

I have two golden rules for hiring:

1. Never hire in a hurry.
2. Never hire to a CV.

When you're preparing for an interview, you need to keep these two golden rules in mind.

Why?

Because when you hire in a hurry (like doing anything in a hurry) there's a good chance you'll make mistakes. When you're desperate, you undervalue the importance of getting things right. In relationship terms, you underestimate your worth, you undervalue what you deserve and, in both dating and hiring terms, you don't wait for your ideal person but settle for the best of a bad bunch – and settling is *never* good!

As for CVs, they're also like profiles on a dating site, written to impress, sometimes exaggerated, sometimes bearing no resemblance to reality at all. That's why the interview is so important. That's why preparation is vital.

You're looking for someone who has the skills you need, who also shares your values, and who will fit the culture of the team you're building. So think about the questions you need to ask to get beyond the CV and uncover the real person. You want to know what makes them tick, what they think is really important, how they feel they can add value to your team.

Open-ended questions are crucial.

- 'Tell me about a time when you...'
- 'Give me an example of when you last had to deal with an angry customer.'
- 'How do you view...'
- 'It says here [on your CV] that you achieved X, tell me how you did that.'
- 'What are you most proud of [in your life] to date?'
- 'What are you least proud of?'
- 'What's most important to you when you're working in a team?'

Hire to your values, not to a CV, and you will have a much better chance of getting the right team member first time.

The first invite to meet the family – their first day

Do you remember when you first met your other half's family? Were you nervous? Well for a new starter – first day on a new job, meeting new teammates, knowing all eyes are going to be on them – multiply those nerves, and hopefully excitement, by a hundred.

I don't know if you remember your first day in a new job – maybe you've had several, maybe you've just had one – but it can often be memorable for all of the wrong reasons.

You know, the manager forgot that you were starting that day and you hear 'Oh, can you just sit there, the manager's in a meeting right now' or 'Oh, you're here. Right. Great. Um, well, nobody's got time for you at the minute, so if you could just sit at this computer and read through our website.' Yes, really! It happens. Way too often.

Then there are the first days that are so uninspiring, dull and boring, that they make your excited new starter feel that they've made the wrong decision, that all of that great stuff they heard at the interview and read in the job ad was just talk.

Do new team members in your business have memorable first days for all the right reasons, or all the wrong reasons? Do they go home inspired, excited and raring to get into day two? Or do they go home feeling unsure whether they should ever go back?

Making a first day memorable is as easy as it's important. Here's how to get it right.

First, you want to make sure that you're fully prepared for your new team member's arrival – just as you might if your new date was coming to your house for the first time. You'll make sure the team knows they're coming, what their name is and what they'll be doing, so that they are prepared to welcome their new teammate.

For their induction, I would always want the business owner (if that's not you) to come and meet my new team member and inspire them with the story of how the business got started, the challenges they've faced, their vision for the future. If the business owner can't be there, make sure you get them to create a simple 'Welcome' video that can be shown in their absence, or sent directly to the new starter's email, to show that they've remembered it's their new employee's first day, and that they care.

In your time with them, you'll share what's important to you and your team, and remind them of the crucial part that they're now going to play in the team's success. You want to inspire them with your plans for them; how you're going to develop them; what the opportunities will be for progression maybe.

Of course, you want to share essential information, like where the fire exits are, where to get their lunch, what they're going to be working on for their first week, but the rest should all be about inspiration and motivation. You want them going home thinking, 'I cannot wait to get started tomorrow', so much better to send them home inspired after half a day, than bored to death after a full one.

- Preparation
- Information
- Inspiration

The three essentials for a memorable first day, for all the right reasons.

Dating – their first 90 days

I'm a big believer that your hiring process doesn't end until your new team member has passed their probation, which makes their first 90 days an essential 'getting to know you, warts and all' exercise – just as it is when you start dating someone.

Less like dating, you want to be really clear, and you want your new team member to be really clear, on what you expect them to achieve in those first three months. What do you want them to have learned? What do you want them to have delivered? What teamwork and personal qualities do you want them to have demonstrated?

During their first week you'll share this with them and then you'll set dates for three important meetings:

- Their 30-day meeting
- Their 60-day meeting
- Their 90-day meeting, which doubles up as their probationary review

These three meetings are as important for you as they are for them. They push you to think about how your new team member is doing – what's going well and what isn't, how you feel they are fitting into the team, what feedback you are getting from the people who are working with them. And what are you going to feed back to your probationer to ensure that they make the grade at their probationary review?

The probation period is often underused, with new team members given an easy ride, sometimes almost forgotten about, as you and your team get on with the busy-ness of your day-to-day work. Probation is there to fully test their suitability for their new role, to test how they perform under pressure, to test if they are a good fit for your team and your culture. So test them. Give your team member tasks that you would normally give to someone experienced, ask for their opinion on how to solve a challenge you're facing, put them under (a little) pressure and see how they react.

By the time you get to their 90-day probationary review, you want to be 100% certain that this person is right for you, and that you are right for them.

And if they're not, don't prolong their probation in the hope that they will become the right person with just a little more time, or because they are 'so lovely'. If they're not right for the role or your team, your gut will have been telling you as much, probably from the first week.

So let them go, with feedback about what they need to work on, maybe about the type of business they will excel in, because they *will* be right for another business. Keeping them tied to your team when they're not right is doing you both a disservice.

A probation period must end with a yes or a no decision – don't fudge it!

Engagement – passing probation

For those who pass their probation, let's celebrate them joining the team, just as you would (or did) with your engagement. Make a big fuss. Give them something as recognition of the big day – a pin, a sticker, a T-shirt, a bottle of champagne to celebrate with their family, and get the team together to welcome their new member. Do *something* to show them that becoming part of your team is a big event.

Then it's all about training and performance management, two areas we'll cover in much more detail in the next two chapters.

Your mission

Create a job ad for one of the roles in your team – getting clear about what you would say in terms of the purpose of your business and the purpose of the role you have chosen. How can you inspire a potential candidate? Then have a go at the pen portrait for the role and get feedback from your boss, or from the team member currently in the role.

If you are recruiting for a new team member, better still!

Taking over a team

Who have you got? How to assess your team

Many new managers don't have the luxury of building their team from scratch. Maybe you've joined a business, or maybe you've been plucked from the very team you're now being asked to manage. So how do you assess your former teammates with fresh, objective eyes?

Well, the first thing to ask yourself is a question I get every business owner to ask themselves: if you could re-hire all of your team tomorrow, who would make the cut?

It's a powerful question, and one that's rarely answered with 'everybody'.

There are often individuals who have never been right; who should have been weeded out during their probation. Others who have never been given the training or, more likely, the feedback they needed, to become a valuable member of the team – remember Anna?

So first, ask yourself the question to identify the person or people who are just not right, because you're the person who's now going to do something about it. (Much more about how to do that in Chapter 4.)

Potential vs Performance Matrix

Next, I want you to plot your team on a Potential vs Performance Matrix. This matrix gets you to assess the current performance of each individual, together with their potential to improve, develop and grow.

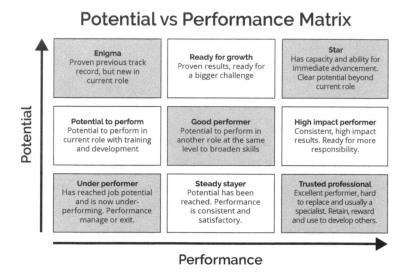

Potential vs Performance Matrix

Enigma Proven previous track record, but new in current role	**Ready for growth** Proven results, ready for a bigger challenge	**Star** Has capacity and ability for immediate advancement. Clear potential beyond current role
Potential to perform Potential to perform in current role with training and development	**Good performer** Potential to perform in another role at the same level to broaden skills	**High impact performer** Consistent, high impact results. Ready for more responsibility.
Under performer Has reached job potential and is now under-performing. Performance manage or exit.	**Steady stayer** Potential has been reached. Performance is consistent and satisfactory.	**Trusted professional** Excellent performer, hard to replace and usually a specialist. Retain, reward and use to develop others.

Potential (vertical axis)

Performance (horizontal axis)

For example, Bill is a good employee, who you can rely on to turn up on time, do his work to a good standard and then go home. He doesn't make any waves, but equally he doesn't contribute anything outside the remit of his role. Bill is happy where he's at and might be described as a Steady Stayer. In bigger teams, these guys are essential.

Meena, on the other hand, is also reliable, does her job to a good standard and doesn't rock the boat, but unlike Bill, she has shown signs that she wants to learn other skills to broaden her knowledge. Meena isn't ready to take on more responsibility, but could move to another team or another role for development. Meena would be classed as a Good Performer.

Sue has only been in your team for a few months, and has only just passed her probation, but you've seen signs that she's going to be good, and you want to give her every chance by giving her the training and feedback that she needs. Sue would sit in the Potential to Perform box.

You get the idea.

Your mission

Download the Performance vs Potential Matrix (via the link in the Resources section) and map your team (however small) into the nine boxes shown. If you work with freelancers, map them in too. You're looking to build a picture of the strengths and the weaknesses in your team, so you need to be as objective and thoughtful as possible.

When you've completed it, book some time to talk it through with your boss to get their perspective and input.

Your people plan

Once you have a clear picture of who is in your team, pull together a people plan that maps out what each individual needs from you, in order to become a valuable team member – what training, what support, what feedback, what performance management?

Are there skills gaps in your team that you need to fill? Can you fill those gaps by training individuals you already have, or will you need to pull a business case together for hiring someone new? How soon will you need to fill the gap you've identified? And what about the team member(s) who need to go? What's your plan for that? Who do you need to speak to? What steps do you need to take? How will you replace their skills/experience?

Your mission

Sit down somewhere, away from distractions, and think this through... carefully. Map out the actions that you're going to take and put deadlines and timeframes against each of them, before presenting your plan to your boss for sign off.

Remember at this stage we're only talking *what* you need to do – the *how* will be covered in the next few chapters.

Understanding your team dynamics

I think you'll agree with me when I say that we're not all the same. We all work in different ways; we all have different styles, different characteristics, quirks and foibles. We communicate in different ways, we want to receive communication in different forms, and we get pleasure out of doing different tasks.

The dynamic within a team affects their productivity, the way they operate and, ultimately, their success. You'll have heard the expression 'being in flow' – in sport it's referred to as 'being in the zone' – meaning the mental state we experience when we are fully immersed in an activity that gives us a feeling of energised focus, full engagement and real enjoyment.

If a team is out of sync or out of flow, things happen slowly or, often, not at all. They are less accurate, they are absent more, they become demotivated – those signs of a poor culture we talked about in Chapter 1.

Different people are in flow doing different things. For example, Manjit might love talking to customers and building warm relationships, while Bill would prefer sitting in front of a complicated spreadsheet looking for the tiny error that he knows is in there somewhere, and Sally is happiest when she's organising something – people, an event; she doesn't care as long as she can have a checklist.

Different people also prefer to get their information in different ways.

Manjit wants to have a little relationship-building chat before you tell him what you need to tell him. Bill wants the facts... and quickly. 'Just tell me what you need to tell me and then go away.' And Sally? Well she wants to know the what, the where and the by when of what you're telling her, so that she can add it to her list and give it the right priority.

Your team are all different, so how can you give each of them what they need in the way they need it? How can you get really clear about who they are and how they operate?

The fastest way I know is through profiling, and the best profiling tool I know is called the Team Contribution Compass (see 'Your mission' at the end of this section) which helps you to understand the profiles and natural energies of the people you manage. While a lot of profiling tools put individuals in a box, the Contribution Compass tool is all about concentrating on, and then making best use of, individual and team strengths, passion and natural talent. It helps each person in a team to understand the quickest and easiest way for them to get into and stay in flow.

The profile assesses personality, strengths, productivity, values and behaviour, which will give both your team and you as manager the opportunity to focus on strengths and to support each other in areas that you aren't naturally drawn to.

Having this information helps you to alter the way you communicate, teach, lead and motivate your team, to get the best possible contribution from each of them. Get this right and you will have engaged team members who love what they do.

Imagine a team that worked well together; a team that could anticipate each other's needs and could back each other up; a team fully 'in flow'. How big an impact could that team have? What could you achieve together?

Building a team who share your values and perform to your high standards is your number one priority as a leader-manager. It's challenging and it can be tough, but whether you are building your team from scratch, or taking over a team from someone else, don't settle for someone who isn't right for *your* team, because you get who you settle for.

Research the Team Contribution Compass at www. mariannepage.co.uk/teamcontributioncompass and discuss with your boss whether it would be right for you and your team.

Chapter 3

Mastering your team's performance

There's only one way to cook French fries in McDonald's.

Training your team is not optional

Every manager wants their team to perform well, to do what they're supposed to do and to the right standard. But do your team really *know* what you want them to do? Do they know the standards you expect? Do they know what 'good' looks like?

The majority of managers I've worked with believe that their team know what to do, and their frustration with their underperforming team is often palpable:

- 'I showed her how to do that two weeks ago, so she should be able to do it without asking questions all the time.'
- 'Everyone knows how to do that – it's just common sense for Pete's sake!'
- 'Why can't they just get it right?'
- 'They're too lazy to even try.'
- 'Can't they work it out for themselves?'

These are all actual comments thrown at me by frustrated managers, and when I ask how much time they have invested in training these people, their frustration only grows:

- 'Do you think I've got time for training? I've so much to do I don't have time to train as well!'
- 'What's the point in training? I can do it quicker myself.'
- 'I'm too busy correcting their mistakes to train.'
- 'I've got my own job to do, I can't be doing theirs as well!'

And so the vicious circle continues.

The truth is though, that without training there can be no consistency, no performance and no ownership. How can there be?

- Your team won't be able to take ownership if you don't teach them exactly what you want them to do and how you want them to do it.
- Your team won't worry about having high standards if you don't give them feedback on their errors and instead correct them yourself.
- Your team won't be engaged in your business if you don't engage with them.

A recent *Harvard Business Review* study revealed that while 36% of business owners expect their managers to develop their team, only 9% actually do. That's a shocking statistic, but not one that you are going to add to.

You're not going to waste the time you've invested to bring the right team together, because you understand that the ongoing, day-to-day development of your team is a major part of your role – something that will not only deliver great results, but also give you a huge return on the time you invest in it.

Let's get to it.

The learning journey

You've probably heard the phrase 'the customer journey', referring to the path your customer follows through your business when they want to buy your product or service. Well, just like your customer, every employee in your business goes on a journey with you that starts on day one and ends on the day they leave you. It's known as the employee journey, but

I prefer to think of it as the *learning journey*, and it has five distinct stages.

1. Memorable first day
2. Orientation
3. First 90 days
4. First 12 months
5. Ongoing training

At each stage of their learning journey, your team member will need input from you in the form of information, training and feedback. You want to be fully prepared to give them all of the right information at the right time. You're building a relationship here – remember our dating analogy in Chapter 2 – so you want to be on your game, professional, prepared for every interaction with them.

Stage 1: Memorable first day

This is your first opportunity since the interview to share information with your new team member – to tell them what the business is all about, the culture, the values, where it came from, why it exists and how much they are going to grow and develop as part of your team.

As we said in Chapter 2, this first day should be 90% inspiration and 10% information, so give them only the information that they have to have on day one and leave the rest to day two and beyond. You want them going home buzzing; knowing they've made a great decision to join you. A memorable first day for all the *right* reasons.

Stage 2: Orientation

This is their first week in your business and you want to make it a good one, so what do they need to know straight away, what do they need to learn, that's going to set them up for success?

You may want them to know how you operate breaks, where most people go for their lunch, what's expected of them in terms of communication with you and the rest of the team. You may want them to pass a health and safety test or understand your fire safety procedures. Or maybe you want them to spend a day in each area of the business, or with each individual if you have a small team, to get a feel for how the whole business operates day-to-day.

Stage 3: First 90 days

The first 90 days, or probation period, is crucial for every new team member in every business. For each role, there will be key tasks that you want your new team member to learn and be able to perform well, in order to pass their probation.

The key to this crucial period in their learning journey is to test them out with some of the more complex and challenging tasks that they will be faced with day-to-day in their role. Don't give someone an easy ride, and then be disappointed when they can't do the job you need them to in six months' time.

These first 90 days give you and your team member the opportunity to work out if you're right for each other, so don't waste them.

Stage 4: First 12 months

Once a team member has passed their probation, there will be more tasks that they need to learn in order to master their role and become a productive member of the team. As their manager it's important that you know what each of those tasks are, and that you map out their development.

Are there tasks beyond their role that you want them to take responsibility for?

Do you want them to learn key tasks of another role to give you cover for holidays?

What do those first 12 months look like for them?

Stage 5: Ongoing training

Team training is an ongoing process. As your business evolves, so will your systems, your products, your needs as a team. With every change, every evolution, every addition to your operation, your team will need training in the *one right way* to perform the new/evolving tasks.

Staying on top of these training needs is a key part of your role as a manager.

Your mission

Look at the learning journey that your team go on – how clear and structured is it? Ask your team members what their first day was like – was it memorable for all the *right* reasons? What can you do to create a memorable inspiring first day? What can you do to improve the structure of your learning journey?

The tools you'll need

The Team Training Map

The Team Training Map is a template I developed to capture the learning journey for every role (or in smaller teams, every individual) in your business.

You'll see below that the template is split into sections which follow the five stages of the learning journey we've just gone through.

Your first task is to identify the different roles in your team. For example, you may have a till person role, a customer support role, a cleaner role, a designer role, an admin role, etc.

As in the example below, the first box will be labelled 'everyone'. This column will capture all of the information and training that you want everyone to have.

Once you have identified the roles, you'll begin to map out the training you want each role to receive, in their first week, first 90 days and so on. Don't worry about duplication of tasks across roles, just capture everything that you want the team member in that role to be able to do in the particular timeframes.

TEAM TRAINING MAP

Everyone	In IRW	[ROLE 1 eg. Admin]	In IRW	[ROLE 2 eg. Ops]	In IRW	[Role 3 eg. Manager]	In IRW
Orientation/Induction							
Welcome to [Business] - Video	☐						☐
Our business culture	☐						☐
Vision & Values	☐						☐
ToV document	☐						☐
Tour of the office	☐						☐
Official Induction (fire safety, ID, forms, handbook etc)	☐						☐
First 30 Days							
	☐	How to revise a document	☐			How to revise a document and ask the right revision questions	☐
	☐	How to use the telephone system	☐			How to review website content	☐
	☐	How to answer the phone (scripted)	☐			How to set KPIs (financial & productivity)	☐
	☐	How to transfer the call to the right person	☐			How to monitor KIPs	☐
	☐	How to record your calls	☐			How to give a Performance Review (share template)	☐
	☐	How to do a risk assessment	☐			How to recruit (HR)	☐
	☐	How to upload a file to Dropbox	☐				☐
2nd 30 Days							
How to answer the phone & take a message	☐		☐				☐
How To put an appointment in the diary	☐						☐
How To send a confirmation email	☐						☐
How To deal with existing clients	☐						☐
Key relationship training & how to deal with difficult customers	☐		☐				☐
3rd 30 Days							
	☐		☐				☐
	☐		☐				☐
	☐		☐				☐

First 90 Days / 6 month Probation Period

*Refresher star each How To for which you'd like to schedule an annual refresher for

62

What you'll end up with is a complete map of the training required for your team, which initially will double up as a list of How To guides/systems that you need to create!

Your mission

Go to the Resources section and follow the link to download your Team Training Map template. Agree a time to sit with your team, to map the training for each role and each timeframe.

Simple logical and repeatable systems

If the mention of the word *systems* has brought you out in a rash, fear not! If it conjures up images of reams of paperwork and box-ticking bureaucracy, think again.

The language of systems – ISO9001, Lean Six Sigma, standard operating procedures, process, protocol – turns an awful lot of managers away from thinking about them, let alone creating them.

And it's unnecessary.

I want you to change the way you view systems, to see them in a different, brighter, much friendlier light. Because the truth is, a system is just a *simple logical and repeatable* way of doing something, and there should be only *one* simple logical repeatable way to do *every* task.

One *right* way.

There's only one way to cook French fries in McDonald's and it's the right way, the McDonald's way. Everybody knows how to do it, and everyone does it this way. No exceptions. No one would dream of doing it any other way.

There's one right way to do *every* task in a McDonald's restaurant – it's simply the way everything gets done. It's these 'systems' that give McDonald's their amazing consistency, make them so reliable, make them so scalable.

Is there one right way to do every task in your business?

If so, great! If not, then we need to look at how you can get to that point, and where better to start than with the How To guide.

The How To guide

The simplest, most straightforward way to create a simple, logical, repeatable system is to create a How To guide (How To, for short) in one of four different ways:

1. The paper-based How To

This is the sort of guide that many people think of when someone tells them to document their processes. It's a written, step-by-step guide to completing a task – step 1 do this, step 2 do this, and so on.

To make this sort of guide effective, there will always be a section at the end of the How To that explains 'why we do it this way'. This serves as both an explanation and a check of your logic, and an answer to the favourite question of many team members, 'But why do you do it this way?'

2. The infographic

This is a visual representation of how the task will be performed. It combines images of the actions to take, with wording for any detail that can't be shown in an image (e.g., a number or a temperature), or to clarify a particular point. A common infographic seen in many businesses is a How To guide for using the photocopier or the printer.

3. The checklist

A checklist isn't often considered to be a How To, but it works well as a summary of How Tos that must be followed in order to complete a bigger task, with tick boxes to ensure that nothing gets missed. A good example of this would be an opening or closing checklist showing things that must be done at the start of every day, and at the end.

A checklist is often associated with several How Tos – for example, if my opening checklist says, 'switch off alarm', I will have either a paper-based or infographic How To showing me how to switch off the alarm.

4. The How To video

All of these versions of the How To are very useful in their own way, and there will be times when only one of the above is practical, but the best version of the How To is everyone's 'go to' in normal everyday life.

Think about it. When you want to learn how to do something new, where is your first port of call?

Google or YouTube, right?

You want to find a video that shows you how to do whatever it is you want to do – boil the perfect egg, wire a plug, create an animated presentation or whatever. A video is the simplest, clearest and most effective way to get a point across, to give information, to explain the what and the why of a task. It's visual, so you can see what's going on, and best of all, you can pause, rewind and go over the 'lesson' as often as you need to, until you are confident you're doing it right.

So your secret weapon when it comes to How Tos will be the How To video.

Now before you start thinking 'No way, I'm not going in front of the camera', or 'I hate hearing the sound of my voice on a recording', two things.

First, you don't have to go in front of the camera, ever, if you don't want to. The idea is that you use screen-recording software to record the task, as you perform it on the screen. You simply talk to the screen telling your team member exactly what they will do, and why it's important that they do it this way.

Second, you will not be the person creating *all* of the How Tos. As far as possible you'll involve your team, getting the people who do each individual task to the high standard you expect to record the How Tos for you.

How To videos work well for 'offline' tasks too. We've had clients create How To videos for dressing bridal suites, setting the building alarm, building a burger, drawing a cartoon, using a machine – you name it, you can create a How To video for it.

Choose one task that you currently perform and create a How To video for it.

The 1RW (One Right Way) Training Tracker

If you want to be sure that everyone in your team has received the training that you expect, you need to be able to track it, and to do that you'll need the 1RW Training Tracker.

1RW is an online platform that we've developed specifically for small successful businesses. It allows you to store all of the How Tos, policies and team information in one place, and assign them to specific roles, exactly as you've laid them out in your Team Training Map. Effectively it creates a learning journey for each role, which you can track and measure.

Once you have assigned a team member their login details, they can then access their training in the set timeframes, monitor their own progress, and even compete with other team members, if you set up the gamification which the system allows.

This is great for your new starters, and also great for team members who have been with you for some time, as it gives you the opportunity to put them through refresher training to confirm that they are following your 'one right way'.

Research the 1RW Training Tracker (1rw.co.uk) to discover how it would benefit your team and help you to track and manage their training.

How to train your team members

Having gone to so much effort to get all of your tools in place, you want to make sure that you get full value from them, and that means knowing how to train effectively.

You may have experienced poor trainers in the past; I know I have. The ones who sit you down, tell you to watch what they do, rattle through an explanation at 100mph, then get up and leave you to it with an 'Ok, got it?' are my particular favourites.

But you're going to train brilliantly, because you've got your How To guides as backup, detailing all the steps to complete and explaining why it's important that your team member follows this *one right way!*

Of course, you probably won't be doing all of the training for your team, but if it's not going to be you doing the training, then you need to train your trainers to follow these steps:

Prepare

Read through your How To guide or watch your How To video to remind yourself of all the key points, making notes if you need to. Double check that you have everything you need to hand, that the equipment is working, that you've allowed enough time, and so on. Be ready to get this right.

ABC training system

Use the 1:1 training system that McDonald's always used to train their team members.

A = Attention

If you want your team member to be listening to what you have to say, concentrating so that they understand and focused so that they are able to act on what they've learned, then you need to get their attention and keep it. There are plenty of ways you can do this, but if you're struggling, try one of these:

- Find out what their existing knowledge is by asking questions – you don't want to be going into detail with stuff they already know.
- Tell them something interesting about the task they're going to learn.
- Tell them a key fact, a funny anecdote or a tale of disaster related to the task.

- Tell them what the benefit of learning this task is for them.
- Let them know how this task fits into the big picture of your operation.
- Make sure that *you're* not distracted and that you won't be disturbed until you're finished training.

B = Breakdown

Decide in advance if the task can be taught in steps (for a simple task) or if it needs to be broken down into bigger chunks of several steps – like building blocks.

Walk your trainee through one chunk at a time, being really clear about what you are doing and why. Think about your pace – too fast and they'll flounder, too slow and their minds will wander.

Get interactive where you can to keep them engaged. For example, 'When you get to this point you do X. Why do you think that is?' This can also be a good indicator of how well they are following what you're saying and if they're making links between one part of the task and another.

C = Check

After every bite-size chunk and once you've taught the whole task, check that they've learned the key elements by asking them a few testing, open-ended questions, starting with what, why, how or when.

If they can't answer the questions, go back to the breakdown and retrain each section until both you and they are confident that they've nailed it.

Practise

Then, when you've finished, let them practise. Think about when you're learning to drive, how important practice is. Well it's no different for your team members – they need to have time to practise, and they also need feedback until they can do the task automatically, following the one right way, and achieving the standard you expect.

As you've probably gathered, I'm not a big believer in over-complicating. This method of training is simple, and it works in the vast majority of situations, regardless of the level of the individual or how complicated the task is. And if done well, it doesn't need to be repeated.

> **Your mission**
>
> Train one of your team members in a new task (or a task where you have just agreed the one right way to do it) using the ABC training method.

Develop for growth

As I mentioned earlier in the book, I was taught that it was my responsibility as a manager to *train the employee* (in the skills they need to do their job) and *develop the person* (helping them to grow in confidence and fulfil their potential) from day one until the day they left and moved on to pastures new.

The best managers recognise that they have a responsibility to help their team members to fulfil their potential, and to do that they have to develop them as people. But how? How do you take raw talent, unearthed potential and develop and hone it into something remarkable?

Well you start with the foundations – training them to excel in their role, to perform consistently, giving them the confidence of a productive and valued team member. Then, onto this foundation of operational excellence, you build their broader skills – the skills that will help them grow as a person. There are several ways to do that.

Delegation

I'd put money on the fact that you've been told more than once, that if you want to have any time at all as a manager, you need to learn to delegate. All too often though, because it's viewed solely as a management time-saver, many managers dump rather than delegate – getting rid of all the tasks they hate, just because they can. We're back to that power thing!

Delegation will definitely save you time, and it will help you to get away from tasks that you don't really need to be doing – that take you out of flow and away from the areas of your job that add most value – but it's also a brilliant way of developing a member of your team and raising their confidence levels by showing that you clearly trust and respect them and their ability to do a good job.

Reasons why managers don't delegate

- **Loss of control:** Often managers won't delegate because they don't want to give up control; they're protecting themselves. They either don't trust the team member to do a good enough job, or they believe their team member may do a better job than they could – and either outcome will make them look bad. These managers clearly lack self-confidence, and miss the point that your aim as a manager is to replace yourself in your current role, to give you freedom and room to grow into your next role.

  I was always taught to surround myself with the brightest people I could – people who were quick learners, smart, motivated, people with initiative – so that I could delegate to them, give them ownership and then get out of their way while they did the job that freed me to focus on the things that fit my skills way better. I love it when my team members are better at certain things than I am. Do you?

- **It takes too long:** Oh if I had a fiver for every time I've heard that! 'I can just do it myself – it's so much quicker.' It's the sort of mindset that holds managers back. Thinking that it's too much effort to give somebody the skills they need to do a job that will save them so much time in the long-term. It's a really short-term view.

- **My team member will resent it:** This is a cracker! Believing that because *you* hate the task that you want to delegate, that your team member will view it that way too, and believe you are dumping it on them. But if you choose the right person – somebody who's brilliant at the task – then that's how you sell the task to them. You can actually say to them, 'I really don't like this task. I can do it, but it takes me a lot longer than it would take you. I know you enjoy this sort of thing and I'd love you to learn how to do this task and take it off my plate.'

It's good to have a team-focused mindset as a manager – to be willing to do jobs that you are asking your team to do. But you've risen to the level of manager because you're good with people, because you're a good leader, because you have skills that other people still have to learn if they're going to grow and develop. Keep that in mind when you come to delegate.

How to delegate
Ask yourself these five questions:

1. Can someone in the team perform this task now, or with training?
2. Is it an opportunity to develop someone's skills?
3. Is it a recurring or routine task?
4. Do I have time to delegate effectively? For example, time to train and give feedback.
5. Is it a task I *should* delegate? For example, you wouldn't want to delegate an interview or a team member's performance review, but most other tasks will be delegatable, if that's even a word.

Once you know you're going to delegate…

- **Choose the right person:** This comes back to knowing your team – their strengths and weaknesses – the tasks that put them in flow, and those that take them out of it.
- **Explain why you're delegating this task to them:** What your reasons are for choosing them for the task, and why are you delegating in the first place.
- **Explain the result that you want:** If you're delegating a routine task, then you will simply train your team member in the one right way to do the task. But if you're delegating something where only the result is important – maybe you want them to organise a team-building event, or create a report, or sort out your stock cupboard – tell them the result that you're looking for and empower them to come up with the 'how' themselves.
- **Make sure they have the resources they need:** Do they need any special equipment or software or team support? Make sure that you set them up for success.
- **Delegate responsibility and authority:** Make sure they know the decisions they can make and those that you want them to run by you. You want them to feel supported in doing the task, but not micro-managed.
- **Give them feedback:** The biggest mistake that most managers make with delegation is not to give any feedback. Always check the work you delegated when it's complete, or at set milestones if that is what you agreed. Make sure it was done to the standard you

expected, and give your team member feedback – either to congratulate them on a job well done, or to help them to improve for next time.

- **Say thank you:** Publicly if it's appropriate; recognising specific things that they did well; showcasing to the rest of the team what good performance looks like.

Use our Delegation worksheet (see Your mission at the end of this section) to support you. It's a simple template that will keep you on top of who you've delegated work to and the results that have been achieved. It will also act as a good reminder of agreed deadlines.

Meetings

How about meetings? How can meetings help you to develop your people?

Well, for a start, you can develop someone by delegating the whole organisation of the meeting to them – the venue, the agenda, the refreshments, etc.

You can then get members of your team to present at team meetings. Getting someone to present to a small group, particularly of their peers, is a fabulous development exercise. Most people fear presenting full stop, and those that can deal with it still feel far more comfortable presenting to strangers than in front of their peers.

Start small, asking each team member to come to your meeting prepared to discuss their area, to share what they feel has gone well, the challenges they've faced since the last meeting, any wins and so on. Get them to stand up when they do their little bit to make it feel like a presentation, give them feedback about how to improve, and over time it will build their confidence and ability.

Most people hate presenting, and don't know how to present well, so by developing your team in this way, you're giving them an invaluable skill for life. Have fun with it!

Mentoring

If you've got somebody who's really struggling in a particular area – maybe they're an introvert and they're struggling to be heard in a noisy team or maybe they're someone with real potential who has a tendency to self-destruct – finding them a mentor outside of the team who's been where they are now, who understands what they are going through, can be a really good way of supporting their development.

Of course, *you* can also be a mentor to individuals in your team. When you see someone struggling, take them to one side, take them out for a coffee, take them for a walk and talk to them about what's going on. 'You just don't seem yourself at the minute. Is everything ok at home? What's going on for you, because obviously I can't have you snapping at me and being sarcastic with your teammates. What you did/said this morning in front of the team – how do you think that made them feel?'

Be a good listener. I don't just mean listening to the words that people are saying, I'm talking about listening for the things that aren't being said – reading between the lines, noticing when people aren't quite themselves. There's a slightly cheesy saying: 'You were given two ears and one mouth, use them in that proportion.' For leader-managers, that is absolutely essential. Don't always be diving in there with what you think, what you believe, what you feel is right. Don't always be in a hurry to get to your solution to their problem. Take the time to listen – that's what a mentor does.

Your example

Remember that you cast your shadow of the leader every single day. Every time you walk into your building, every time you pick up the phone to one of your team members, every time you're on a video call, every time you write an email; however you interact with your team, you are casting your shadow over them and they feel your presence.

Whether it's the superhero presence, 'Come on! We are a team. We can do this.' Or whether it's 'Oh Lord, s/he's in such a bad mood today. This is going to be the day from hell', is up to you. Choose wisely.

Don't be the manager whose team are on tenterhooks every day waiting to see who's going to turn up. Choose to be consistent. To be consistently positive. To be consistently firm, fair and friendly with your feedback. Choose to be the example that you want your people to follow, because you *are* the person they model and mimic, for good, bad or ugly. They watch you and they copy you – so give them the best version of you every day!

Mastery of your team's performance is an ongoing task for every manager, but with the right mindset, and the right foundations in place I have no doubt that mastery is exactly what you will achieve!

And when you do, watch your team fly!

Your mission

Download the Delegation worksheet I mentioned earlier, following the link in the Resources section. Consider the tasks you could delegate now, and the tasks you could delegate with training. Delegate one of your existing tasks to one of your team.

Chapter 4

Mastering feedback

You get the standards you tolerate.

I'm a big believer that the purpose of feedback is to inspire and motivate someone to improve their performance.

Feedback should never leave somebody feeling down, feeling like they're no good, like they're never going to get any better. Feedback should always inspire improved performance – even if it's marginally improved performance, there should be some movement forward.

So how do you achieve that? How do you give that sort of feedback? That's what I want to cover in this chapter.

- The importance of giving feedback.
- Who to give feedback to.
- How to give feedback that inspires.
- How to receive feedback and what to do with the feedback you receive.

I think it's fair to say that as a nation, the British are pretty rubbish at giving feedback, and as a result we often don't get the outcome we are looking for.

We use sarcasm, which can go straight over the head of the person we're talking to.

We use humour, which can downplay the important point we're trying to make.

We avoid giving any feedback at all whenever possible.

All of which means that the situation continues, and nothing improves.

Why managers fear giving feedback

- You are not taught how to give feedback, so you don't have a strategy for doing it well.
- You don't give feedback often enough, so you have to build up to every feedback conversation.
- You believe that it's demotivating to give feedback when the team, or an individual, is working really hard, is under pressure or maybe even has challenges at home.
- You fear the reaction. What if they get angry? What if they get emotional? How will I deal with their response?
- You believe that you can't give feedback to people who used to be your peers, because you'll come across as bossy or on a power trip.

Any of those ring a bell?

If so, it's important to remember why you were chosen to be a manager, and the responsibility that comes with being a manager:

- To improve performance.
- To develop your team.
- To help individuals to reach their true potential.

Which, coincidentally, are the three main reasons for giving feedback. So let's tackle the main reasons for your fear and give you a strategy for doing it well.

Four types of feedback

First of all, let's look at the four types of feedback.

1. No feedback

The most common type of feedback is giving no feedback at all. Every day in every business, managers are walking past problems in their team, ignoring poor standards, not commenting on things that are being done well. This is by far the worst type of feedback because it shows a lack of care and leads not only to a deterioration of standards, but also to the team disengaging. 'If you don't care, why should we?'

2. Negative feedback

Negative feedback is where you launch into somebody, tell them everything that they've done wrong but don't actually share with them how to put it right – usually doing it very loudly, quite aggressively and most often in front of the rest of the team.

Any improvement as a result of negative feedback is rarely long-lasting. In fact, the most likely outcome is a long-lasting negative feeling towards you. As you walk away, the person that you've just given negative feedback to is not thinking: 'Alright, so I need to do X, Y and Z to make sure I get this right next time.' Instead they're thinking what a proper piece of work you are. They're thinking about you, not how to improve their performance.

If you're looking for confrontation, negative feedback – or pure criticism as we should rightly call it – is the way to get it.

3. Constructive feedback
Constructive feedback is where you tell somebody what they haven't done to standard, and then, crucially, you tell them what they need to do to put it right, how they need to improve their performance, what they need to do differently. It's fully focused on achieving a positive outcome – the improvement of your team member's performance.

4. Appreciative feedback
Appreciative feedback is where you tell somebody what a great job they've done, picking up on the specifics of what made it such a good job, so that they can continue to achieve this standard going forward.

Create a learning environment

When you are learning something new, you expect to be given feedback. Whether you are learning to drive, learning to play the saxophone, learning to cook, whatever the new skill might be, you expect to be told what you're doing wrong, and how to do it right. You recognise that feedback is crucial to your development. You know that if you want to master your new skill, you need to listen and respond to the feedback that you're being given.

This expectation of training and feedback is known as a learning environment, and it's an environment that you want to create within your team. Just like you, when you learned to drive or bake or play the guitar, you want everyone in your team to expect to be given effective training, and feedback that ensures they keep learning and developing their skill.

When you've created a learning environment, day-to-day feedback becomes the norm, so there's no fear of it, whether you're the giver or the receiver.

How to give non-confrontational feedback

The strategy that makes me comfortable when I'm giving feedback has three elements that vary only slightly depending on whether I'm giving appreciative or constructive feedback. I use it at work, at home, in restaurants – whenever I need or want to give feedback.

1. Tell the person why you're speaking to them. What you have seen or heard. What you asked your team member to do and how they did it. What the reason is for you giving them feedback.
2. Tell them the effect that what you have seen or heard has had or will have – on you, on the team or on the business.

3. Tell them what you want them to change or continue to do. With constructive feedback, you'll tell them what you want them to do differently to meet the required standard. With appreciative feedback you'll tell them what you want them to continue doing, to reinforce their good performance.

An example of constructive feedback might be:

> Sue, I've just listened to you answering the phone. You answered it within three rings which is great, but remember to use your name to make it more personal and warm, like this, 'Good Morning Acne Consulting, you're speaking to Sue, how can I help you today?' And let's hear that smile in your voice. We want the customer to want to do business with us, so we need to make them feel really welcome. Ok?

Constructive feedback is always focused on the bit of someone's performance that you want them to change or improve – giving them all of the information they need to do just that.

An example of appreciative feedback might be:

> Well done, Gail, you answered the phone really well there. You made the customer feel welcome, you gave your name to make it personal, and I could really hear the smile in your voice. Loved it! Keep doing exactly that.

This feedback strategy is simple, and it works because it's focused on specifics. Specifically what you saw or heard.

Specifically what you want your team member to do differently to improve, or to keep doing. It's also completely focused on behaviour and not on personality.

What do I mean by that?

Behaviour vs personality

As a manager you can't change someone's personality (according to one study that's pretty much fixed at the age of five), but you can observe someone's behaviour and then give them feedback which allows them to change it.

We want to give feedback that's focused on how someone has behaved, rather than *who someone is,* in other words 'You did' versus 'You are'.

Here's a few examples:

- Personality focus: 'You are so rude.'

  Behaviour focus: 'You've interrupted me three times during this conversation, which makes me think you're not interested in what I have to say.'

- Personality focus: 'You've got a really bad attitude.'

  Behaviour focus: 'When you roll your eyes and sigh when teammates suggest ideas, it makes me think that you don't respect them, and it could lead to them not speaking up in future.'

- Personality focus: 'You're incredibly selfish.'

Behaviour focus: 'I've noticed that when a teammate is struggling you don't do anything to help them, even when you are on top of your own work.'

- Personality focus: 'You're very irritable today.'

Behaviour focus: 'You've snapped at me and your teammates several times today – is everything alright?'

When to give feedback

- When you're training someone.
- When your team member has completed a task you delegated to them.
- Any time you spot behaviour that doesn't fit your team's values.
- Any time you see someone deviating from the one right way to do a task.
- Any time you see something that's a great example of the values and standards you expect.

In other words, every time something needs to be said, say it – and go looking for opportunities every day!

Your mission

Find an opportunity *today* to give one piece of appreciative feedback, and one piece of constructive feedback. And don't worry if you're not at work today – this strategy works brilliantly with friends, family and total strangers too!

Share the love

In most teams there are three types of people:

1. **The choir** are the people in your team who are the real superstars, they are the people who you love having around you – your high flyers. They're the people that you give the big jobs to with confidence that they'll get them done.
2. **The crypt** are the people who are underperforming; people who are either constantly moaning or constantly asking the same questions over and over again. They are very high-maintenance, although not always through their own fault.
3. **The congregation** who sit between the choir and the crypt are very often forgotten because they are steady, they are reliable, they are consistent. They don't ask for anything, they are possibly never going to be your high flyers, but they are absolutely solid as a rock. You know that they will come in, they will do a really good job and then they'll go home. No trouble, just really consistent, steady team players.

What percentage of your time do you think you spend on each group – your superstars, your underperformers and your steady reliable team members?

Perhaps your choir, your superstars, don't need too much of your attention because by definition they are self-starting high achievers. Your time is spent with them on public praise and in high energy gatherings, on setting new challenges and keeping them stretched and fulfilled. After all, you want to keep them!

What about the crypt? People in here may just need to be trained and nurtured to progress to the congregation or even the choir. But how much time and energy do you spend on someone who you know is just not the right fit, because you dread having that conversation with them, so you put it off? How often do you find yourself ranting about them and what they've done to your friends or at home?

What about the person who does an ok job but who is incredibly needy of reassurance, of constant encouragement, who picks on any little thing, who sucks the life out of you on a daily basis? How much time do you spend and how long do you persevere?

And then how much time does that leave you to spend on people who simply do their very best every day – the congregation? They may not be superstars in the recognised sense of the word, they may never achieve greater wealth or status than they have already, but they go about their work cheerfully every day and they do it consistently well.

They are the sort of people who you would want beside you in the trenches; the sort of people who are calm and measured in a crisis, who have had their share of hard knocks but just keep bouncing back; the sort of people you can rely on to be… well, reliable! Good, solid employees who possibly have great potential, but you're not even seeing it because of your crypt and your choir.

Think about that. Think about who is hogging all of your time because the truth is, every one of your team members needs feedback to stay engaged.

Common mistakes managers make when giving feedback

- Pre-empt any feedback with 'Do you mind if I give you some feedback?' If you've created a learning environment, you will never need this phrase anyway.
- Use the phrase 'constructive criticism'. The word 'criticism' is inherently negative and that's usually how it is then received, regardless of how constructively it's given.
- Focus on constructive feedback and give little, if any, appreciative feedback. If you never praise anyone for a job well done, your team will start to believe that they simply can't meet your standards, and may stop trying. If you've given constructive feedback on a Monday and by Friday you've seen the person responding positively to the feedback you gave them, really trying hard to deliver in the way you wanted them to deliver, then give them some appreciative feedback to show them that you noticed.
- Have a room that you take team members to, to deliver your constructive feedback. In my early days with McDonald's this place was always the stockroom and being taken to the stockroom became something everyone dreaded. Certainly you should take someone away from their colleagues if you're delivering feedback about their behaviour, but if you have created a learning environment, and simply want someone to adjust/ improve how they perform a task, you don't want to take them too far from their workspace to do that.

91

Feedback is the cheapest, most powerful and sadly the most underused tool that you have in your management toolbox. It keeps everyone's performance on track, keeps your standards high and keeps your team engaged and motivated. Make sure that you use it. Daily!

Giving formal feedback

Creating a learning environment and giving your team effective, day-to-day feedback is definitely more important for team engagement and performance than your formal performance review system, but there are a number of very good reasons why formal performance reviews are still essential for your business.

- They are a great opportunity to review goals and to challenge your team members with new ones.
- Employees want to know where they stand and want to have their performance formally assessed and reviewed by their manager. It's *their* time with you, and it's precious to them.
- They are great for building rewards around.
- When things go wrong, they are essential in managing someone out of the business who has stopped performing.
- They are a great two-way communication tool.

I've always recommended that managers commit to quarterly performance reviews using a simple one-page review document like the one below.

Quarterly Performance Review

NAME		REVIEW PERIOD	

Performance Reviews exist to celebrate the areas in which you excel, or perform well and to discuss how best to improve those areas which require improvement. Performance development is your personal responsibility. Your reporting manager is here to support you and encourage you not only to achieve the standards expected, but to fulfil your full career potential.

BUSINESS ASSESSMENT	EXCELLENT	GOOD	SATISFACTORY	NEEDS IMPROVEMENT	UNSATISFACTORY
Demonstrates professional competency and knowledge in day to day work					
Takes full ownership for, and builds strong Customer Relationships					
Follows 'new customer' process consistently					
Completes all work accurately and on time					
Follows daily processes and routines consistently					
Pays particular attention to proactive communication with customers					
Applies training and uses initiative to pre-empt/resolve issues					
Enters all appropriate information accurately into filing system					
Keeps other team members informed of work which may affect them					
Takes ownership of Personal Development					
TIME MANAGEMENT & PERSONAL ORGANISATION ASSESSMENT	EXCELLENT	GOOD	SATISFACTORY	NEEDS IMPROVEMENT	UNSATISFACTORY
Performs well against monthly team targets					
Achieves customer turnaround times consistently					
Sets and regularly achieves challenging personal targets					
Consistently performs well against recoverability targets					
Responds to customer e mails/ telephone messages within 4 hours					
Manages workload well to deliver on targets					
Asks for help if needed to achieve deadlines for customers					
TEAM CONTRIBUTION ASSESSMENT					
Communicates well with other team members					
Is a positive influence on the atmosphere within the office					
Keeps other teammates motivated when the pressure is on					
Helps other team members when needed					
Shows a desire to achieve the best possible outcomes for our customers					
Communication is clear and consistent (oral and written)					
Listens effectively and asks for clarification when unsure of what is required					
Contributes positively to team meetings and 1:1 meetings					
OVERALL ASSESSMENT					
ADDITIONAL FEEDBACK					
IS THERE ANYTHING I/WE CAN DO TO MAKE YOUR LIFE EASIER?					
REPORTING MANAGER SIGNATURE			EMPLOYEE SIGNATURE		

Visit the Resources section for the link to your downloadable template.

This one-page review covers three key areas of performance:

- **Business assessment:** How well is your team member performing their role? Are they contributing to the business? Are they good with your customers? Do they always follow the one right way to do every task?
- **Time management and personal organisation assessment:** Are they meeting deadlines? Are they prioritising their work effectively to get everything done? Are they responding to colleagues and clients?
- **Assessment of contribution to the team:** Do they help out their teammates? Do they keep others motivated when the pressure is on? Do they contribute to the team?

In each area, you have the opportunity to rate your team member on a number of specific points, all of which can be adapted to suit your team and, if necessary, the different roles they perform. Giving each point a rating, which ranges from Excellent to Unsatisfactory, creates the discussion and gives you the opportunity to give very specific constructive and appreciative feedback.

The most important thing to remember when it comes to a formal performance review is that nothing you say to your team member should be a surprise. Nothing. Ever. Your quarterly performance review should simply be a summary of their overall performance based on all of the individual pieces of feedback that you've given them over the past three months.

The very best managers keep a record of the ongoing feedback they've given, so that they can use specific examples of the behaviours they want to comment on in the formal review. Something for you to consider, maybe. It's certainly a good habit to get into.

When you first start doing your quarterly performance reviews, you'll find that it's you who will do most of the talking. Over time you want that to change, you want to create that learning environment we talked about where your team are taking control of their own development; where they're coming to their performance review talking about what they believe they're doing well, what they feel they need to improve on, the support that they need from you in order to improve and get to where they want to be.

You want to be the person listening – that's when you know that you've really achieved a learning environment, and also a high performing team, because your high performing team members will want to take control of their own development and their own performance improvement.

One way to encourage this is to give each of your team a notebook called 'My Development Diary', where you ask them to record what they've done well since their last review, what they've learned, any praise they've received, anything they'd like to do for their own development and anything you could do to help. It's a great tool for helping your team to reflect and learn, and of course they can refer to it during their review, which will build their confidence.

The second most important thing to remember about performance reviews is that there have to be consequences – for good performance and for performance that isn't up to standard.

If there are no consequences for the poor performers, the standard of your best performers may well start to drop off. They'll start to feel neglected, unrecognised; to feel like, 'well, what's the point? I'm working like a Trojan, I'm doing a fantastic job. I know I'm doing a great job. And Bob over there is coming in, doing the bare minimum, going home dead on the dot, and we're being treated in the same way. It's just not right.'

There need to be consequences. Performance measures for those who need them, and rewards for those who deserve them.

Don't always think that rewards have to be monetary either, there are plenty of other ways to acknowledge your brightest and best team members and their contribution to the team – giving them greater responsibility, maybe the opportunity to attend a conference, to get additional training, perhaps even promotion to the next level.

Whatever you do, make sure you have consequences for those who are not performing to your high standards, those who need serious improvement, those who are no longer a fit for your team. Do something to improve them or move them on.

In summary

- Make your feedback inspiring and motivational.
- Give it as close to the event as possible.

- Build a learning environment where giving feedback is 'the way we do things round here'.
- Talk about specific behaviours, not someone's personality.
- Focus on the fix – make your feedback all about helping your team to improve their performance.
- Listen to what they have to say about how you can support them to improve.

Remember: you get the standards you settle for.

Your mission

Download the one-page performance review (via the Resources section) and set aside some time to adapt each section for your team. Where necessary, e.g., for a very specific role, create a separate version, to make it as relevant to the role as possible.

How to receive feedback

Are you open to feedback – from your team, from your boss, from clients?

Do you recognise that you don't have all the answers? That you don't always get things right? That, just like your team, you can learn something new, and improve your performance, every single day?

I know that when I was a fresh-faced young manager, back in the day, I didn't get it at all. I felt I had to be right all of the time – I believed I was right most of the time – and I didn't take feedback well. My mindset around feedback was all wrong.

The truth is that feedback is a gift.

It may not always be packaged well – not everyone has learned about the difference between negative and constructive criticism – but it's always a gift because it gives you choices…

- Accept the feedback and act on it.
- Accept the feedback and don't act on it.
- Discount the feedback and do nothing.
- Accept the feedback, and dig deeper to learn more.

What I learned about myself in relation to feedback, was that while I didn't always receive it well initially, I would always go away and think about it. I'd reflect on what was said, I'd analyse how valid it was, and I'd make a decision to act on it or not based on a thorough examination of the facts.

If you recognise that the feedback given to you is valid, great. Accept the feedback and adjust your behaviour to benefit from it.

If you've been given feedback that you really disagree with, go back to the person who gave it and talk it through – explain your thinking, your alternative view, because the truth is that those of us who give feedback are not always right either. Sometimes we give feedback based on limited data, so it's important to create a culture where somebody can challenge us, can challenge our feedback and say, 'Thanks for your feedback. I've really thought about what you said, and I'd just like to take you through what I've learned – I think it might change your opinion.'

When you've developed that sort of relationship with the person that you report into, and when you've built that sort of relationship with those who report into you – where you're able to challenge one another constructively – that's when great things will start to happen in your team.

Feedback opens new doors, it starts discussion, it adjusts mindsets and it brings about positive change.

Your ability to master the giving and receiving of feedback will have a huge impact on your success as a manager.

Your mission

Think of a time you received feedback recently – how did you react? Were you defensive or did you accept the feedback with thanks and reflect on it? How could you benefit more from the feedback you receive?

Chapter 5

Mastering your communication

What do your team want from their manager? Consistent, regular, honest communication is top of the list.

Whenever I go into a business and talk to the team, one of their biggest complaints is always about communication – that they aren't communicated with effectively, that they don't know what's going on, that they're kept in the dark. When they're given information, it's often too late or missing important details.

To be seen as a great communicator by your team is crucial for any manager, and it's essential for keeping your team engaged. But what is engagement?

For me, your team are engaged when they have real enthusiasm for their work and are emotionally committed to your team and its goals. When your team are engaged, they don't leave you, they are way more productive and they take ownership for their role.

As I said in Chapter 4, feedback is the cheapest, most powerful and sadly the most underused tool that you have in your management toolbox. It keeps everyone's performance on track, keeps your standards high and keeps your team engaged and motivated.

Unfortunately there's plenty of research out there that tells us less than a third of employees *are* engaged, and that managers, and the way we communicate, are largely to blame.

Obviously, that's not good.

It means that if you don't master your communication skills, you will have little chance of engaging your team. And if you don't engage your team, then every day could be a struggle.

How to keep your team engaged

The current state of play

As recently as 2019, TINYpulse (a leading employee engagement platform) completed a survey of over 200,000 employees, from over 20 different industries, in businesses ranging from 10 to 10,000 employees, to understand the current level of engagement. Their research delivered six key findings and they don't make good reading:

- Employee engagement is decreasing – 43% of workers would be willing to leave their companies for a 10% salary increase.
- Leadership teams lack self-awareness – while 39% of managers strongly agree that communication within their business is transparent, only 22% of employees feel the same way.

- Employees need better direction – less than half of employees feel that their promotion and career path is clear to them, with a staggering 44% of employees feeling that they don't have enough opportunities for growth and development.
- Employees aren't getting the recognition they deserve – only a third of employees received recognition the last time they went the extra mile at work and just a quarter feel highly valued at work.
- Employees care deeply about their colleagues – 91% of people rate their colleagues positively, and yet just 9% of people think their average teammate is very happy.
- The number one factor that predicts performance is the level of support provided by managers – while high performers rate the level of support they receive at 8/10, low performers rate it at 6/10.

What keeps an employee engaged?

The Towers Watson study

A major US consulting firm, Towers Watson, have been studying employee engagement for more than a decade now, surveying tens of thousands of employees across the globe in the process. Their findings are enlightening for every manager in every business.

Just look at those statements! Every one of them (well, maybe with the exception of 'I have a best friend at work') gives you the opportunity to make a major impact on engagement. Every one of them relies on the quality of the communication skills we're going to master in this chapter.

What Makes an Employee
Highly Engaged?

Proportion of highly engaged employees experiencing this

Proportion of low / no engagement employees experiencing this

Highly Engaged

92%	Someone has talked about their progress	13%
97%	Someone encourages their development	10%
88%	They have been praised recently	13%
98%	They have opportunities to learn and grow	13%
74%	They have a best friend at work	19%
98%	Their manager cares about them	20%
98%	They view their job as important to the business	22%
91%	Their opinions count at work	19%
93%	Their team mates are committed to quality work	44%
99%	They are able to do their best every day	53%
98%	They have the equipment they need to do their job	70%
99%	They know what is expected of them at work	89%

Low or No Engagement

Towers Watson Engagement Survey

As manager of your team you can talk to an individual about their progress and encourage their development. You're in a position to give them opportunities to learn and grow, and to keep the whole team on track in delivering quality work. It's within your gift to listen to their opinions and to show that you care for them as an individual.

The power to keep your team engaged is in your hands. How good does that make you feel?

Common mistakes

To master your communication and become a better manager, it helps to be aware of the common mistakes that will block trust and engagement between you and your team.

Here are the seven most common mistakes managers make.

Mistake 1: Not communicating enough

One of the biggest complaints I hear from teams is that they are not kept informed of what's going on in the business, with many managers believing that information should be given on a 'need to know' basis. What they miss out on by keeping their team in the dark is the trust that comes from transparency, and the engagement that comes from a belief that we're all in this together. Open communication really is essential to building a successful team.

If you want to know what to communicate and what not to communicate, ask yourself these questions:

- Is it confidential (like competitive information maybe)?

- Is it personal (for example, to an employee)? *Never* gossip with your team!
- Is it harmful (to an individual, for example)?

If the answer to all of those questions is no, then share the information with your team. Especially valuable to share is information such as:

- The goose-bump-giving business vision that you want the team to buy into.
- Plans for the business and your team, long- and short-term.
- Progress that the team is making down to the smallest of wins.
- Information that will build people up, not put them down.
- Information that tells them how they are doing as individuals and as a team.

Mistake 2: Underestimating your team's knowledge and ability

One of the biggest mistakes I see managers making is to treat their team members as if they are stupid, lazy and occasionally belligerent children. Remember I told you back in Chapter 1 about the guy on LinkedIn who was telling any manager who would listen to him that that is exactly what employees are. And how wrong he is.

Whether you have hired well (to your values) or not, I believe that everyone who comes to work with you is full of potential, has their own motivation and is usually smart (whether that's street smart or educationally smart), and it's up to you to engage them in a way that draws the very best out of them. Treat people like stupid children, and they will usually behave that way. Treat them as the bright and capable adults that they are, give them the training that they need, and they will blossom and shine.

Mistake 3: Lying

Let's be honest, we all know that managers lie to their employees all the time. Little white lies and big fat porky pies. And this lying is very much linked to Mistakes 1 and 2 – trying to hide the truth from the team and treating them like children.

Lying is a dangerous game for a manager to play, regardless of the motivation for doing it. Lies have a way of being uncovered by your very smart team, and there is no quicker way to lose trust and respect than to be caught in a lie.

Every team values a manager who is straight with them – who they can rely on to tell them the honest truth, and not sugar-coat feedback or bad news, a manager who delivers on their promises. When you tell somebody straight what the situation is, or how they need to improve their performance, you give them a chance, and the choice, to think and act for themselves.

Mistake 4: Being unapproachable

Many managers wrongly believe that to be a good manager they have to be aloof from their team – remember the peacock! Some go on a power trip, barking orders before disappearing behind a closed door, not to be disturbed, leaving their team floundering and too afraid to ask for help.

As a communication strategy, this is disastrous. All of the communication is one-way – from you to the team, and certainly not delivered in a productive manner. Problems and challenges are left unresolved because your team don't see the point in raising them and, over time, your operation becomes increasingly inefficient and dysfunctional.

Mistake 5: Being too approachable

On the other hand, it's also a problem to be there to answer every question and give the solution to every problem. You want your team to think for themselves and you also want to protect your own time while giving your team the time and the input they need.

We'll talk a lot more about this in Chapter 7.

Mistake 6: Overusing email

There are two major issues with email communication between a manager and their team.

One is overuse. In general, managers send way too many emails and, worse still, they expect an almost immediate response, regardless of the day or time it is sent.

The second issue is that weaker managers hide behind email rather than being straight and having that honest conversation we were talking about a minute ago.

We all know the communication problems that email can cause, with even the most carefully crafted email being misinterpreted and not received as the sender intended it. As a result, email bullying (intentional or not) is a very real threat in every workplace, and it's up to you to make sure that you don't go down this path.

It's up to you to create a culture of open and honest face-to-face communication.

Mistake 7: Believing that 'I sent an email' is enough

A third issue with email is a manager over-relying on an email to get their message across to their team, or an individual within it. Not following up to check that the message was received at all, let alone as intended. Not taking into account possible technology glitches, or an email getting lost in someone's overfull inbox. Not understanding the communication needs of different individuals in their team.

So many problems are caused, and deadlines missed, as a result of this one mistake alone.

Email is good as a backup to face-to-face or telephone conversation, but in a highly engaged team, it should never be the only method of communication used.

How to communicate

Ok, so we know now what not to do. Let's turn our attention to how to communicate well.

We talked in Chapter 1 about the shadow of the leader; about how all of your communication – everything you say, and don't say; everything you do, and don't do – is being observed, received and acted on by your team.

How you show up every day, how you respond to challenges and complaints and stressful situations, how true you stay to your stated values in what you say and do, sets the tone for your team and, over time, builds your team culture.

So it's pretty damn important that you're constantly focused on communicating well.

No pressure then!

How to become a great communicator

Communicate in line with your values

What on earth does that mean?

Well, if values are the things that are most important to us about how we want to operate and live our life – the compass that guides all of our decisions, behaviours and actions – then I'm talking about communicating in a way that stays true to what's important to us.

- Maybe it's being kind.
- Maybe it's always being straight with people.
- Maybe it's always trying to find win-win solutions to problems.

Sounds like it should be easy, but of course it isn't. We all do things at times that go against our values and leave us feeling cross with ourselves. You know, you wanted to be kind but then you found yourself gossiping about someone and laughing about them behind their back. Or you had the opportunity to help someone with some really straight-talking feedback, and you fudged it, laughed it off, let them carry on underperforming.

When you do something that goes against your values, you feel it in your gut. I bet you've caught yourself saying 'It just didn't feel right' or 'I knew I should have listened to my gut' – well, that's your values talking, so listen to them, because when you communicate in line with your values, you feel really good about yourself.

Learn to be more self-aware

You can't really be a good leader if you don't know yourself; if you don't know what your values are, what you struggle with, what your triggers are, what gets you 'in the zone'. Being self-aware helps you to be true to yourself, to be more open and authentic in your communication, to understand your successes and failures, and what you need from your team to complement or make up for the skills you have or don't have.

So how can you begin to develop this awareness?

At least once a week, take time to think and reflect. I know, it sounds almost too simple, doesn't it? It's a lesson I learned some time ago from a fellow business owner. He told me that every week he set aside 90 minutes to reflect on the previous seven days, asking himself questions like:

- What was I aiming to achieve?
- What went well, and why?
- What didn't, and why?

- Did I do anything or say anything that wasn't in line with my values?
- What lessons have I learned about myself this week?
- What am I going to do better next week?

Of course, most managers don't take time to think – some might even consider this sort of exercise a waste of valuable time. But the investment of that 90 minutes, or even a third of that time, once a week, could be the difference between being an average manager and a great leader-manager. I'd say that makes it worth the effort.

Listen more than you speak

Remember: 'You have two ears and one mouth so use them in that proportion'. Be the manager who listens more than they speak. All great communicators listen to their team, giving everyone the opportunity to share their opinion, their knowledge and their experience, making sure that any introverts in their team are not drowned out, watching for non-verbal clues as well as what is said.

Being known for your willingness to listen brings you closer to your team; it shows you care about them as individuals and their input to the business. When people feel appreciated in this way, they're more likely to respect *your* opinion, which gives you greater influence as a manager.

Listening to your team gives you the chance to catch potential issues before they become big problems. It helps you tap into your team's energy and notice when someone needs input, or a figurative arm round the shoulder, or some training. Every aspect of your role as a manager will benefit from your efforts to become a better listener.

The following tips will help you to listen well.

- Be attentive and completely engage in the conversation. Stop looking at your screen, put your phone where you can't be distracted by notifications, and *never* look over the other person's shoulder to what's going on behind them, or look at your watch. (I'm sure it's not just me who gets really annoyed by that one!) If now is not good for you, agree a time for your team member to come back.
- Listen to the body language as well as the words. Look for clues as to how they are feeling. And watch your own body language too – keep it open and maintain eye contact.
- Repeat back the gist of what you hear, to confirm that you've been listening, and that you've understood the point your team member is making.
- Ask questions to clarify your understanding. Make sure that you haven't just taken the words you heard at face value. Ask questions until you're certain that you've fully understood the meaning behind the words.
- Think before you speak and don't shoot from the hip in a way that may come across as reactive or dismissive. Be measured in your response, and if you want more time to think things through, agree a time to get back to them.

Admit when you don't know something or when you're wrong

Few managers want to show vulnerability, but owning a mistake or admitting that you don't have all the answers will actually grow your respect with your team. It's back to that 'being straight with people' thing. If you're honest, say you don't know something and ask for their help to work out the answer, you'll be amazed at the number of brownie points that earns you with the team.

Ask for feedback

'What can I do better to help you improve your performance?' is a great question to ask your team members, particularly during performance reviews and one-to-ones. How can I improve? What can I do better? What blocks can I remove that will help you to operate more efficiently/give our clients a better service?

These questions all show your team that you care, that you know you're not perfect, and that you value their opinion. Of course, you then have to reflect on and respond to their feedback, acting on it whenever possible.

Have some fun

Just because you're a manager doesn't mean you have to stop having fun. Some of the most productive teams I've ever worked with put having fun right up near the top of the agenda, and there are loads of studies out there that will tell you that a happy team perform way better than an unhappy one.

What can you do to bring some fun into your workspace?

Know your people

Remember back in Chapter 3 I said that you should train the employee and develop the person from day one? Well, it's also important to get to know the person from day one and to be prepared to communicate with them about their life beyond work.

Talking to your people about the things they care most about – their children, their pets, their car, their football team – showing that you're not just interested in what they can do for you and the business – allowing them to bring a little of what they love into the workplace – inspires much greater engagement in your team.

Be kind

In these days where kindness is at a premium, be a kind communicator. Be firm, be straight as we've said before, but also be friendly, consistent and above all fair, finding win-win solutions whenever you can.

Be consistent

Being consistent both in terms of what you communicate and how you communicate will win you an awful lot of respect from your team.

- Communicating consistently about the key focus for your team – where you're headed, what your three big goals are this year/this quarter/this month, what progress you're making, what's working, what's not.

- Communicating with clarity – keeping things simple, keeping your communication regular. Communicating with confidence.

When you are consistent in the what and the how of your communication, your team know where they're at and are able to work productively with confidence in your leadership, knowing that if there is something they need to know, you'll tell them.

Consistency is crucial.

How to communicate with a virtual team

When it comes to engaging a virtual team, or even one virtual assistant, remember that they have many of the same communication 'needs' as your in-house team. They still need to be listened to, to know how they're doing, to feel valued as a member of your team and so on. But of course, as a manager, you need to make much more of an effort to keep them included and involved.

The conversations you can have, and the feedback you can give 'in passing' to a member of your in-house team day-to-day, are not available to you when your team member is remote, sometimes on the other side of the world and in a different time zone to you.

So it's really important that you agree set protocols for how and when you'll communicate, and then be disciplined in sticking to them.

Technology has made the world very small and is definitely your friend here. How easy is it to jump on a video call, sharing files and presentations, seeing and hearing the other person as clearly almost as if they were sitting in the same room. Channels like Slack and WhatsApp are also helpful in keeping information flowing between all members of the team. And of course, the telephone still works too!

As far as possible, you want to treat your virtual team member in exactly the same way as your face-to-face team members – same performance measures, same goals and deadlines, same communication.

How to communicate change

In every business, things change, stuff happens, and it's your role as a manager to keep your team up to speed with what's going on, to manage the change so that they aren't unsettled by it, and to keep everyone positive as far as you possibly can.

Communication is everything when it comes to managing change. Here are six top tips for getting it right:

1. Be very specific and very clear about what is changing, and why.
2. Think about who might be affected emotionally by the change, and speak to those team members individually.
3. Tell your team the good news – what's in it for them, what the benefits are of changing. And if there is no

good news, tell them that too, and thank them for their patience while you do what has to be done.

4. Paint a clear picture of what will happen when, and manage their expectations in terms of any timeframes.

5. Make it clear what, if anything, you need your team to do and get them involved whenever you can.

6. Give anyone who has concerns the opportunity to come and talk to you one-to-one.

As a manager it's always important to communicate clearly and honestly, but during uncertain and unsettling times of change, it is essential.

How to communicate with your boss or your team through a presentation

In terms of communication mastery, your ability to present to a group is not as crucial as, say, your ability to give constructive feedback, but it's a great skill to develop, not least because it's a massive confidence booster when you do it well.

I could write a whole book on presentation skills, but for now I want to share just three key things that I want you to work on.

1. Preparation

As with your meetings, planning and preparation are everything when it comes to presentations. Ask yourself:

- What's the point of my presentation? What are the (maximum) three key messages I want to get across?

119

If my audience were to walk away with only one key message, what do I want it to be?

- Who am I presenting to? Are they interested in what I want to talk about? What would spark their interest?
- What questions will they ask? What will they challenge? Put yourself in the shoes of your audience and make sure that you have the answers to the questions that you know they will ask.
- Keep your presentation simple and brief.
- And practise. Test your presentation out on a colleague, or at home with family or a friend you know will give you good feedback.

2. Delivery

When I was learning to present, I was always told to structure my presentation into three parts:

- Tell them what you're going to tell them.
- Tell them.
- Tell them what you've told them.

It's a very simple structure, but it's one that will serve you well, particularly as you're developing your presentation skills. Beyond that, your preparation and practice will give you the confidence you need to deliver well.

3. Questions

If you've done your preparation well, you'll be ready for most questions that are thrown at you. But if you're asked something that you haven't thought of and you don't know the answer, admit it, say that you'll find out and get back to them, and then make sure that you do.

Never try to bluff and bluster your way out of a tricky situation, just stay calm, stay confident and if there's a lesson to be learned for next time, learn it!

To be a good manager, a manager who connects with and engages their team, you must first master your communication skills, and then build a rhythm of communication that your team can rely on. That's what we'll be covering in the next chapter.

Your mission

Communication is a constant thread that runs through every element of your role as a manager, so how good are you as a communicator, and what do you need to improve? Go back through this chapter and choose one aspect of your communication that you are going to work on this month. Share what you are working on with your boss, and the team if it's appropriate, and ask them for feedback at the end of the month. Pick another for next month, and the month after, and so on. Make it a regular habit to always be working on an element of your communication. It's really *that* important.

Chapter 6

Mastering your team's rhythm

The beat that drives your team performance.

L ife is full of rhythm. The sun rises and sets, the tides ebb and flow, the seasons come and go, even if not as consistently as they used to! We have rhythm in music, rhythm in poetry, rhythm in sport. And of course, we have rhythm in business – rhythm that ensures what's supposed to happen happens when it's supposed to – rhythm that keeps your operation flowing and drives operational excellence.

As the manager of a team, you are crucial to your team's rhythm. You set the pace. You synchronise your team's activities. You maintain the discipline of your routines – keeping everything consistent and reliable.

Think about the conductor of an orchestra, or the cox in a rowing team, or the central midfielder who dictates the speed and rhythm of the team's play – that beat, that rhythm, that pulse, is essential to the success of the performance, to the quality of the end result.

Within every team, there are three key elements that you have influence over, which will create and maintain the rhythm of your team's performance: your planning cycle, your communication system and your routines and rituals.

Your planning cycle

I appreciate that not everyone is a fan of planning. It often takes way too long to pull a plan together, and then it's often filed away and forgotten about. I get that. But nevertheless, I'm a very big fan of 90-day planning and goal setting, because even if you don't create an action plan for each goal and even if you don't work your plan, there's a huge amount of power in thinking through what you want, where you want to get to, and getting what you want to achieve in the next 90 days down on paper.

I love the 90-day planning cycle!

We all have a really good feel for what we can get done in 90 days – how much progress we can make towards our big goals. The 90-day cycle gives a team great rhythm, providing focus and energy and also that sense of accomplishment as you achieve wins big and small and drive on to the next challenge.

Working with 90-day goals keeps us focused, keeps us moving forward, keeps us agile and on our toes, and gives us the chance to tackle challenges and grab opportunities as they come along, adjusting our plans for the next 90 days to accommodate them.

I talk to business owners a lot about the importance of having a regular planning cycle. It's something that has been key to the consistent and continuing growth and success at McDonald's. Leaders at McDonald's have a clear business vision and they develop goals for the next three years that will take them towards that vision. They then set goals for the next 12 months that will take them towards their three-year goals. Before finally, and rhythmically, developing 90-day goals that will ensure that they achieve their 12-month goals.

Every 90 days, every manager in McDonald's gets their team together to review what's been achieved in the quarter, and plan for the next. It's a wonderfully rhythmic activity – consistent, regular as clockwork, reliable – that keeps everyone in the business focused on the vision and on track to play their part in its delivery.

Of course, as a manager within your business, you may not be setting the vision, but you do have a key role to play in setting 90-day goals for your team, ideally in collaboration with your boss.

How to set your 90-day goals

1. Meet with your boss to agree what the priorities are for your team for the next 90 days. If they give you a big long list of goals, ask them to prioritise it, to

help you understand what is most important to them. Make sure that you know what their three biggest priorities are – the goals that you and your team absolutely must deliver – before you end this conversation, and confirm what you've agreed at this meeting in writing.

2. Before meeting with your team, spend some time thinking about your goals, and the role that you want individuals in your team to play in delivering them. Get really clear in your own mind about the best way to achieve your goals, but stay open to your team's input and ideas.

3. Meet with your team to share your goals and to discuss your plan for delivering them. Begin with the biggest priorities and for each one agree all of the individual actions that need to be completed in order to achieve the goal, who will be responsible for making sure that each action is completed and when each action will be completed.

   • Some of the actions may need input from more than one person, but always have just one person as the 'owner' of the action. Remember how we talked about developing your team by giving them extra responsibility? Well, this is an example of doing just that – giving one person responsibility for getting a task completed by a mini-team within your team.

   • Be clear and firm with your deadlines – challenging, but realistic should be your mantra. You're setting the pace here, don't forget, so you want to make sure that you set a brisk one that keeps your team productive and on their toes.

4. Before you end your planning meeting, agree dates for your next 90-day meeting, and also your goal review and update meetings at 30 and 60 days, which will play a big part in maintaining your rhythm.

> Your mission
>
> Set a date to meet with your boss to agree the priorities for your team and set your 90-day goals.

Your communication system

Closely allied to your planning cycle is your communication system, in fact they're completely interlinked. You agree the plan, you communicate the plan, you follow up at regular set intervals to ensure that the plan is being implemented day-to-day, week-to-week, month-to-month in a rhythm of continuous forward momentum.

Sadly, regular meetings get a bad name; you may recognise a few of these statements:

- I hate meetings they're so boring.
- They take up way too much time and we don't have time.
- They wouldn't work with my team.
- Meetings are just an excuse to chat.

- We see each other all day anyway.
- There's only a few of us.

How to run effective meetings

One of the best opportunities you have to communicate with your team as a group is through a meeting. But how do you keep the team engaged in your meeting and how do you make sure that you're using the time it will take to hold your meeting effectively?

As with many things in business, the key to a successful meeting is planning.

A really good way to get focused for your meeting is to ask yourself six questions starting with why, what, when, where, who and how.

Why are we having a meeting?

- Do we really need to meet at all? What are the benefits of meeting? What are the downsides, including cost?
- Is there a better way? Could we have a call, use video or simply exchange emails?
- If only a few individuals are involved, might it be more effective and cheaper to talk to them individually?

The answers to these questions will depend largely on what it is you want to talk about, and the size and geography of your team.

What is the purpose of the meeting?
Start with the end in mind.

- Is it a regular weekly/monthly meeting to review the achievement of targets and progress towards goals?
- Is it a meeting called to discuss a particular issue or challenge for the team?
- Is it a meeting to share information with the team and get their feedback?

Be clear about exactly what you want to have achieved by the end of the meeting.

Be specific, for example:

- Everyone will understand the issue and will have been involved in developing a solution.
- We will know what actions we are going to take, and who will be responsible for them.

- Deadlines will have been agreed.
- We will know how we are going to measure progress.
- We will have a record of the agreements and actions from the meeting, to be distributed.

Who needs to attend?

Don't drag people into a meeting 'just for their information', unless that is the whole purpose of the meeting (for example, a team communication meeting).

Ideally you'll invite:

- Those who are directly involved and will be responsible for taking action.
- Someone to manage the meeting and someone to take notes of agreements and actions.
- No more than seven attendees. Too few and it may not be worth using a meeting for the issue; too many and it will drag on as everyone has their say.

When is the best time to meet?

This may come down to when people are available but if there's a choice, pick a time when people are most focused and energised.

Avoid first thing in the morning as your team may be distracted as they come into work and need time to settle.

Lunchtime meetings can work well, as long as you provide food, or tell the team to bring their own food in for a working lunch.

Don't have meetings in the hour before your team normally go home, as they'll be tempted to shorten any discussions, or not give input they would normally give, for fear of not getting away on time.

Mid-mornings probably work best, once your team have had their caffeine shot and are more 'into' the day.

Where will we meet?

You may not have many options here, but ideally somewhere quiet where you won't be disturbed. If you have nowhere in-house, and want to keep your costs down, then a quiet area of a café will work, with the white noise masking your conversation. Again, it depends on the number of people you have in the meeting and what its purpose is. For short meetings like a daily huddle, you'll simply find some standing space near to where the team are working.

How will we run the meeting and how long should it take?

A well-controlled, effective meeting will have a start and end time, and will stay on track throughout. Sounds easy, but we all know it's not!

The following tips and tricks may help you:

- The average attention span is about 40 minutes so keep meetings as short as possible.
- Stand rather than sit to stop general chatter developing.
- Circulate a meeting plan and any reading material before the meeting (if you wait until the meeting to do this, you will waste valuable time as everyone reads what you've given them).

- Ask those attending, and anyone who should attend but can't make it, to send through any comments or questions in advance.
- Set the meeting at five minutes off the hour or half hour and start on time even if someone hasn't turned up.
- Keep a watch on the table in front of you and don't let people ramble.
- Ensure no one dominates and everyone has their say.
- Make sure everyone has their mobile phone switched off and that any laptops are kept closed.

By the end of the meeting your aim should be to have achieved what you set out to achieve, with everyone feeling that they've been heard, and fully committed to the agreements and actions, even if they didn't fully agree.

Always spend the last few minutes of any meeting confirming the actions that have been agreed, who they have been assigned to and what the deadlines are. And make sure that your note-taker has a record for circulation to everyone who needs it.

Then it's all about your follow-up!

Your mission

Download these documents – Meeting Plan example, Meeting Plan, Agreements and Actions (via the Resources section) – and use them at your next meeting.

Meetings that will give your team rhythm

The daily huddle
Short and sharp, and a great way to keep everyone engaged and involved.

Who should attend: Everyone in the team (if you have remote workers get them to join on Zoom, Skype, etc.).

Length: 10 minutes max.

Purpose: To have the team share what they're going to achieve today and commit to it.

What should each team member share?
- What's my focus for the day?
- What's my target/goal?
- Where I'm stuck and may need help.

If someone is stuck then they should stay behind after the huddle to either get immediate support, or agree a time when this can be discussed further.

Where and when: Same time and same place every day, and standing, so no one gets too comfortable, or distracted.

Start on time regardless of who's there.

What to record: There's no need for an agreements and actions sheet, but I've seen many teams write their commitments on a whiteboard – top three things I'm going to get done today – and then review them in an end-of-day huddle. Even without the end-of-day huddle, this can be a very effective way of getting people to do what they say they will.

The weekly team meeting
A more formal review of what's been achieved in the week, and preview of the coming week's activity and goals.

Who should attend: This depends on the size of your team. Usually the whole team unless your team is divided into mini-teams, in which case you'd probably want to meet with the mini-team leaders.

Length: 60 minutes max.

Purpose: To review the past week and set up for success in the week just starting.

What should each team member share?
- How have we done against our targets for the week?
- Did we do what we said we'd do?
- My wins this week.
- My lessons learned.
- What progress have we made towards completion of our assigned actions on the 90-day goals?

What should you share? The results of the whole team, with public praise for any wins.

Where and when: Same time, same place every week.

What to record and share: Agreements and actions.

The monthly team meeting
A more in-depth look at what the team has achieved, and how they have performed over the month.

Who should attend: The whole team.

Length: This depends on the size of the team, and whether or not you will incorporate any training, but usually half a day.

Purpose: To review progress towards the team's 90-day goals, reset for the next month, and share any input from the business owner if they are not present.

What should you share?
- Progress towards the 90-day goals.

- Areas where the team haven't delivered for discussion about lessons learned and how we're going to improve going forward.
- Wins to celebrate.
- Broader information about the business results and an update on the bigger vision and plans.
- What's coming up in the next month and how the team can continue to improve results.

Where and when: Ideally same time and same place each month.

What to record and share: Updates to your 90-day plan, plus key agreements and actions.

The 90-day planning meeting
A key meeting in the team's calendar four times a year, with the last meeting doubling up as the annual planning meeting, and team celebration!

Who should attend: The whole team.

Length: A full day if possible. If not, two consecutive half-days.

Purpose: Review and celebrate the last 90 days, and set the plan and priorities for the next.

What should you share?
- What has and hasn't been delivered against the plan.
- Wins to celebrate.
- Plans and goals for the next 90 days, agreeing who, what and by when for both the goals and the tasks associated with delivering them.
- Opportunity to have your boss share broader information about the business results and update on the bigger vision and plans.

Where and when: Ideally away from the office.

What to record and share: Your next 90-day plan, plus any other key agreements and actions.

In summary

Can you see how these meetings build rhythm in your business, keeping everyone focused, informed and moving beat by regular beat towards the achievement of the team's goals?

- The annual meeting sets the direction and prioritises the goals.
- The 90-day meeting chunks the big goals down into achievable smaller goals.
- The monthly meeting makes sure that the team haven't gone off track and are still focused on priorities.
- The weekly meeting measures and monitors progress.
- The daily huddle keeps your finger on the pulse, highlighting and giving you the opportunity to remove any blocks for the team, or any individual team members.

Now I'm pretty sure that you, or if not you your boss, will be asking, 'Sounds great, but where is all this time coming from for these meetings? It's a big investment for us.' And you're right, of course, there is a cost in terms of both time and money.

But I want you to consider the findings of recent research by Gallup, which revealed that teams who score in the top 20% in terms of engagement have 41% less absenteeism, 59% less turnover and are 21% more profitable than other teams.

Engaged employees show up every day with passion, purpose, presence and energy. These meetings involve your team, give them ownership, hold them to account, show them that their contribution to business success is essential and also valued. Engagement, and all of the positives that come with it, is the powerful return on your investment.

Your mission

Consider which of these meetings would have the biggest impact on communication between you and your team. Trial the daily huddle for one week and assess its value with your team at the end of the week.

Your routines and rituals

Routines

Routines are a part of business life, and a really great way of building rhythm. They help you get things done that need to be done at a set time – every day, every week on the same day, every month and so on – and they give you and your team the structure you need to perform efficiently and effectively.

Team routines are a good thing, so what are we talking about here? Well, the team meetings that we've just gone through are one, very important, set of routines to create, and I'd recommend you start there.

After that I'd focus on your *operational routines*:

- What time of day do you plan for the next day, what day and time do you plan for the next week?
- What day and time do you do your ordering (stationery, supplies, etc.)?
- When do you complete your weekly and monthly KPI reports?
- What day do you deliver your weekly team report to your boss?

Your start-of-the-day routine

If you work in an office or have your own building, then your routine may be to work through an opening checklist – switch off the alarm, turn on the lights, turn on the photocopier and check the paper stock, etc.

It may be to have everyone arrive 15 minutes before the start of their shift, so that they're ready to start work when they're meant to, and aren't still getting a drink or eating their breakfast.

Maybe you want to encourage a routine where everyone works on one of their priority tasks for the first 90 minutes of their day and doesn't check their email until this task is done.

Think about what you want done at the start of the day and work with your team to create the routine.

Your end-of-the-day routine

As above, what do you want your team to do at the end of the day? Do you have a closing checklist? How do you want your team to leave their desk/workspace or the kitchen area? Again work with the team to create a routine that is respectful of their work environment and each other.

What do you want the team to do at the end of the day in terms of their work? Mark commitments off the board? Maybe you want everyone to spend the last 15 minutes of each day reviewing what they've achieved and planning for the next day.

Download our Routines spreadsheet (via the Resources section) and capture all of your routines. Involve the team to make sure you capture those you already have and create a few new routines that would help your rhythm.

Rituals

Rituals are similar to routines in that they're regularly repeated, but they're different because they are activities that demonstrate and reinforce the key values of your team. Phrases like 'it's what we do here' and 'oh, it's a [business name] tradition' are clues that you're talking about rituals.

Rituals help to develop your culture, to engage your team, and because they're regularly repeated, they're a familiar and rhythmic part of the business.

One business I know has a couple of rituals that many teams would love. They start their week with Monday omelettes and end the week with Friday evening champagne. Another (a manufacturer of beautiful leather jackets) has a ritual of giving every new starter a leather jacket on the day they pass their probation. Of course both businesses are pretty successful and can afford to invest in rituals like this, but rituals don't have to cost money at all.

Here are a few rituals that you could create for your team.

Milestone celebrations

An example of this might be to link your 90-day planning and goal review meetings with pizza for the team – so your ritual would become 'planning and pizza'.

Other milestones to celebrate would be work anniversaries – at McDonald's we used to receive something to mark our first, third, fifth and tenth anniversaries.

And then of course there are birthdays. You may already mark these with the time-honoured ritual of the birthday girl or boy bringing cakes for the team.

Turkey of the week

Sports teams use this ritual sometimes – marking something funny or daft that someone did during the week or month by giving them a rubber turkey, which they then have to keep with them until somebody else receives the award. You have to know your team really well for this one, and never use it in place of giving constructive feedback!

Superhero of the week

As above but for somebody who's done something special, either for the team or a customer.

Ring the bell

If you manage a sales team you could introduce the ringing of a bell or a hooter when one of the team signs up a new contract.

First-day ritual

Taking a new starter out for lunch on their first day or when they pass probation is a lovely ritual to have. It's also good to show the new team member how much you value the people in your team.

Monthly lunch-and-learn sessions

Another great one for showing the team how much you care for them as individuals. You have to do them right though – interesting topics that most of the team (it doesn't have to be all of them) will benefit from; a good speaker (not someone who reads from a slide deck); no more than 40 minutes so that they still have time for a breath of fresh air.

In summary

Rhythm is essential for you, your team and the business you all work in. It's essential for every team.

A successful rowing team works together to the same rhythm. They have their oars in the water at the same time, and their oars out of the water at the same time, with the cox key to making that happen.

A successful orchestra plays to the same rhythm and beat, with every musician looking to the conductor who is key to making that happen.

A successful farmer understands the rhythm of the seasons and how to work with them – when to sow, when to reap, when to plough, when to farrow – year after year, with a steady beat.

It's so much easier to swim with the tide than against it, so much easier to sell ice cream in summer than in winter, so much easier to build a high performing team when you have a 90-day planning cycle in place, when your communication system is consistent, regular, expected, and when your routines and rituals create the comfort and certainty within your team of 'this is who we are', and 'this is how we roll'.

Master your team's rhythm, and consistent, continuous improvement is what you'll deliver for your business.

Your mission

At your next team meeting, talk to the team about rituals. Ask them if they recognise any you have unconsciously created already. Think about other rituals you may want to create to build both your rhythm and your team spirit.

Chapter 7

Mastering your personal management system

Put your own oxygen mask on first.

I've been there as a manager, and I'm sure you have too – having so much to do that you do nothing, other than stress about it. So much work piling up that you can't concentrate on the task in hand.

How often do you hear yourself say, 'there just isn't enough time in the day to get everything done that I need to'?

Once a week? Once a month?

How often do you get to the end of the day wondering where your time went, feeling frustrated that you didn't achieve what you set out to? Or miss deadlines that your boss set you, or that you set yourself?

How many times have you let friends or your family down because you were 'just too busy' to stick to plans you'd made to spend time with them?

Your personal management system

One of your greatest challenges as a manager is protecting your own time and energy. There's so much for you to keep on top of – your new team need your input and support, your boss has things they want you to do, and then of course there's your own work that still needs to be done. So how do you keep all of the plates spinning – keep all of the balls in the air – and still have a life? It's a balancing act that many managers fail to master because they start with the mindset that everyone else comes first.

No. It doesn't end well that way. Remember what they tell you in the safety briefing every time you fly – always put your own oxygen mask on first!

That doesn't mean you don't support and develop your team, and it definitely doesn't mean that you ignore the needs of your boss. What it means is that you develop a personal management system that protects your time, protects your energy, and allows you to get your work done – to give what you need to give to your boss and your team, and still have a life.

Sound good? Well let's get into it then and deal first with something that may be affecting you right now… overwhelm.

How to get past overwhelm

I'm sure that you have days where you feel overwhelmed – where you can't see the wood for the trees, where your to-do list for the day is so long it will take you to the middle of next week just to get through half of it.

As one-offs, these days are manageable – there are simple tools and techniques to get you through them, to deal with them and still get stuff done. But it's when these days start to merge, when as one manager said to me, 'overwhelm becomes the norm, when you forget where the hell you're going, let alone how you're going to get there'.

That's when overwhelm has become a real issue.

And that's when you need to complete the 'My Big List' exercise.

My Big List

1. Decide on the timeframe that's overwhelming you. Is it what you have on today, tomorrow, the coming week, the coming month?
2. Next, get yourself a big sheet of paper and a pen and write down everything that you believe you have to get done in that time period.

3. Write down everything – and I mean *everything* – you believe you have to get done in the coming week; personal, business – everything!

4. Once you've done that; once you've exhausted everything, and you're sure you have it all on that sheet of paper, grab a big black marker pen.

5. Go through your list and cross off everything that doesn't move you towards what you're trying to achieve; everything that doesn't move you towards your 90-day goals; everything that isn't important to your personal relationships. Be ruthless here, look for other people's priorities on this list and get them crossed off. Look for things that are easy to do, but are just feeding your inner procrastinator – like setting up a to-do list app, or reading through all those emails you've subscribed to – and get those crossed off too. Cross off anything that doesn't move you to where you know you want to be. *Ruthless* is the key word.

6. There will be things on your list that do have to be done, but don't have to be done by you; things you have on your Delegation worksheet from Chapter 3. These things get moved onto a second list, called 'to delegate'. Add all the things that need to be done, but not by you, to this list. Recognise those things that you may be busying yourself with that are not moving you or your team, or your personal relationships in the right direction.

What you are left with after this exercise, are three lists:

- Your **Do** list – the things you're going to do because they move you towards the achievement of your 90-day goals, including your own personal goals.
- Your **Ditch** list – full of other people's stuff, and things that you've just got into the bad habit of adding to your list every day.
- Your **Delegate** list – things that you're going to get other people to do.

Do, ditch or delegate!

Give this exercise a go next time you feel overwhelmed. I promise you, it works like magic.

You have to be ruthless though, and you have to get over your guilt about ditching other people's priorities – just remember that that's what they are, other people's priorities, not yours! You have plenty of your own to be getting on with.

How to prioritise

Once you have your reworked list of things that are important for you to do, you need to prioritise them, because – believe it or not – everything does not matter equally.

When I prioritise I use a tool called the Eisenhower Matrix, or more commonly, the Urgency vs Importance Matrix, which helps you to get really clear about what you must do and in what order.

As you can see, the matrix has four boxes to hold your tasks.

URGENCY VS IMPORTANCE MATRIX	
Plot your to do list on this matrix to help you prioritise and boost your productivity	
IMPORTANT but not urgent	URGENT and IMPORTANT
Spend time over these tasks and do them carefully	Do these tasks now and do them thoroughly
Do not waste any time on these tasks	Do these quickly to get them done
Not important and not urgent	URGENT but not important

In the top left we have the box for *important, but not urgent* tasks. Here you will put things like setting the dates for your team's next round of quarterly performance reviews or putting the agenda together for your next monthly team meeting or delegating one of your tasks to a team member.

All of these tasks are very important – you want to spend time on them and do them carefully – but they're not urgent and you don't have to get them done right now!

In the top right is our box for tasks that are *important and also urgent,* so they need to be done now, and they need to be done thoroughly. A client has complained about one of your team and has asked you to call him – urgent and important. The deadline for giving your monthly report to your boss is tomorrow morning – urgent and important. You've scheduled time for training one of the team in a key task and need to prepare – urgent and important. Or maybe it's a 'frog task'! You've probably heard of the expression 'eat the frog', where the frog is the task you really have to do, and really don't want to do – something that you dread doing and have been putting off – sooner or later, your 'frog task' will sit in the important and urgent box.

These tasks are your most immediate priorities. Do them now and do them well!

Bottom right is for tasks that are *urgent but not important*. These are tasks that you need to get done and done quickly, often because they are in one of your team's or your boss's urgent and important box. Perhaps one of the team is organising the Christmas party and is waiting for you to decide what you want off the menu. Often it's an email that's popped into your inbox, where the sender (maybe your boss) is demanding an immediate response – even though, in the scheme of what you have to get done, responding is not important, it's clearly urgent, so you'll respond and get it out of the way.

The final box is for tasks that are neither important nor urgent. To be honest, if you've completed your Big List, you won't have anything left that fits this box. If you haven't done the exercise effectively, you'll have things like 'check social media', 'read emails I've subscribed to' or 'set up time management app'!

Don't waste your time here – it's way too precious.

As Eisenhower said: 'What is important is seldom urgent, and what is urgent is seldom important.'

Complete the Urgency vs Importance Matrix once a week, to set your priorities and focus on what's really important for you and your team. Once you've completed it, I want you to ask yourself two questions every day.

First – 'What are the three things I must get done off the matrix today?'

Then – 'If I can do only one thing – what would I want it to be?'

I want you to be going home happy, thinking: 'Yes, it was really important that I completed that task [or ideally those three tasks] and I did it – it's done, off my list, and I'll sleep easier tonight knowing that.'

Remember your rhythm

In Chapter 6 we talked about the importance of rhythm and the benefit of getting into routines that keep everything consistent, reliable, expected. We talked about planning your

90-day goals to keep you focused on what's really important, month-to-month, week-to-week and day-to-day.

Planning is a vital part of your personal management system. Investing time in planning each and every day is crucial not only to you staying proactive and on the front foot, but also to you protecting your time and energy.

I talk a lot about starting your day *on purpose* – knowing what you want to achieve (your three things or your one thing), understanding how what you achieve today will move you one step closer to achieving your 90-day goals and your goals for the year. Too many managers (and business owners to be fair) let the day happen to them, and then feel frustrated when yet another day has passed them by without anything being achieved.

Don't be that manager.

Plan your week either at the end of the previous week, or better still, invest 30 minutes on a Sunday evening to work out your priorities, and decide what you absolutely have to get done, and what you're going to get done, by the end of the week. Then, every evening, invest another 10–15 minutes, planning the next day so you hit the ground running, clear about what your *one thing* is going to be, and confident that you're going to achieve it, regardless of anything that might derail you or hit the fan.

The small investment of time in planning will save you heaps of time every day and every week, and it will also help you to sleep better knowing the next day is planned before you switch off.

Batching for improved focus and productivity

Multi-tasking is a lie! There – I said it.

Man, woman or beast, it makes no difference, everything you ever learned about the benefits of multi-tasking is just not true.

We can *do* two things at once, but we can't *focus* on two things at once. If you were talking someone through landing a plane, you'd stop walking. If you were walking across a tightrope, 30 feet in the air, you'd stop talking. It makes sense. Focused effort gets more done in less time than switching between tasks, and there've been a whole host of studies done that prove that point.

So how do you stay focused?

One of my top tips for productivity is batching, or pulling similar tasks together, and doing them all in one time period – like the way most people do their household shopping. They create a list of all the things they need, decide on the food they want to eat in the week ahead, add in any little luxury extras, and then go and do the weekly shop, or put in the weekly online order. They don't go to the shop every single day to get food for that evening, or to buy washing powder one day and toilet roll the next.

Why?

Because it's a waste of time and energy, and it would stop them from doing other important things in the time it would take them to go backwards and forwards to the shop.

Rather than flitting from one task to another, having to refocus every time you change task – from something creative, like writing a blog maybe, to something that requires more analytic thought like pulling together a report, to something that needs you to be in a different headspace altogether, like making client calls or doing team PRs – batching allows you to get in the right mindset for what you've set yourself to do, to get 'into the groove' as you're doing it, and to increase both your productivity and the quality of your work as a result.

For you as a manager, batching is all about gathering similar tasks together, and doing them all within a set timeframe, without any distraction to maximise your focus and your productivity. It could mean batching together all of your number crunching and reporting in one time period; batching your team member training sessions together two or three times a week; preparing your team one-to-ones in one batch of time, and completing them one after another in a different batch of time; batching calls to clients; batching your email answering.

One thing to watch for with batching is matching tasks to your energy, or staying in sync with your productivity clock, as I prefer to call it. I'm a morning person for example, and I know that I'm at my brightest and best first thing, so if I'm going to work on my financials (which I need more energy for) then I'll plan that into my day early so I know that I'll be sharp and on it, and also that when it's done, I'll still have a good chunk of the day to do something more creative and fun, something that I naturally have more energy and enthusiasm for, like writing content for a blog… or a book! If I scheduled my financials in for mid-afternoon, then no matter how hard I tried, my brain would struggle to focus, and it would take me longer to get them done.

Growing up I remember that everyone was expected to be productive at the same times during the day. And we just aren't. There are early birds and night owls, and every shade of grey in between. Everyone has a natural rhythm so you need to work out what yours is, if you don't know already, because working against it will ruin your productivity and could lead to you burning out long-term.

Teach your team how to work with you

An awful lot of managers, new managers in particular, believe that they have to be available for their team every minute of every day. They've heard how good managers have an open door policy, and they don't want to shut their door and turn the team against them. I worked with a young manager last year who was really struggling to achieve her own goals and was working ridiculously long hours, because she was allowing her (even younger) team to come and interrupt her whenever they had a question – and they seemed to have a lot!

'Oh Jill, can I just ask you a quick question?'

'Jill, can I just get your opinion on something?'

'Jill, can I just…?'

If this rings a bell for you, then the first thing I want you to do is think about the questions you are being asked, and ask yourself a couple:

- A. Is there a training need here? Do the people who keep coming to me with questions not know the answers because they haven't been trained well, or at all? Or…
- B. Is there a confidence issue? Does this team member know what they need to do and how, but just want the reassurance of always double-checking with you?

If your answer is A, it's a training issue, then clearly you need to set aside time to do some training or delegate the training to one of your trusted senior team members.

If your answer is B, then there are two parts to your strategy for dealing with these interruptions:

Part 1 is to get your team together and tell them that you're happy for them to come to you with questions and problems, but that you will only listen to them if they come to you having thought through possible answers or solutions for themselves.

You will then listen to their problem and possible solutions, and ask for their recommended course of action, giving them feedback on their thought process, and building their confidence by praising them for coming up with the right answer for themselves.

Over time you'll notice that they only come to you with real challenges, and even then that they've already worked out the best way to deal with them.

Part 2 is to set aside a couple of hours in the day (say 10–11 and 2–3) for 'team time', where individuals can come to you with any questions they have, or challenges they are facing with their work, or maybe outside of work, that are affecting them personally. Issues or blocks raised in the daily huddle can also be dealt with here.

Setting aside this time for the team gives you control, allows you to manage your time and protects both your energy and your productivity. 'Team time' also keeps that door open, and shows the team that while you may not want them to interrupt you when you are focusing on your work, you still want to give them the support they need on a daily basis.

One additional benefit is that trivial issues are dealt with by team members who don't want to wait for 'team time' to bring them to you.

Both of these strategies will take time and discipline to embed into your culture. You're not going to stop the 'Can I just…?' questions without real effort. But set your stall out clearly – no problems without solutions, and most questions and challenges raised at 'team time'. Educate your team in the benefits to them of working in this way, and you'll soon find that your team start to think for themselves way more, and rely on you as the fount of all knowledge, way less.

How to get control of your biggest time vampire

Don't be ruled by your 'ping'!

The biggest time vampire for managers is their inbox. So many managers lose whole days in their inbox. You know what I'm talking about – you plan your day, have it all set out the evening before, and then the first thing you do in the morning is check your inbox. You see something in there that belongs in the *urgent, but not important* box – an email from a client, or your boss, or one of the team – and you dive right in – react, react, react – and when you next look up, most of your day is gone! Your inbox has completely derailed your day, and you blame what was in there for the frustration you now feel having not achieved what you set out to... again!

The truth is though, when you lose your day to your inbox, it's on you. You've allowed yourself to become a victim of the biggest time vampire of them all – and you're not a victim, so let's give you back control.

Reframe

The first thing I want you to do is reframe the way you think about your inbox. It's not necessary to answer your emails in a millisecond. What would happen if you were on a day off, or in an all-day meeting, or ill, or somewhere with terrible Wi-Fi? There is very little that is life and death or business-threatening in your inbox, nothing that can't wait an hour or two, some things that would benefit from you sitting on them, thinking them through, and not leaping in with an immediate reaction or overreaction. If something was that urgent, you'd get a call.

Switch off your notifications

Second thing – switch off your notifications. Very difficult for you if you like to feel connected all the time, but worth it if you're looking to protect your time and be more productive. Notifications are the 'Can I just...?' interruptions we just dealt with, only in electronic form, so we need to deal with them in the same way.

Check and deal with emails twice a day

Remember your batching, and set two time slots a day, maybe 11–12.30 and 3.30–4.30, where you check and deal with your emails. Put an automated message on your email that tells anyone who contacts you, 'Thanks for your email, please be aware that I only check and answer my emails twice a day, so please be patient, I will get back to you.' And then stick to it. Be disciplined. You don't need to be in there all the time, reacting, reacting, reacting.

Follow the four folder strategy

When you are working in your inbox, ask yourself these questions:

1. What does this email mean to me and why do I care? Is it important to me?
2. What action do I need to take? Do I need to take any action?
3. What's the best way to deal with this email and its content? Do I have to do anything?

Then based on the answers to these questions, put each email in one of these four folders:

Folder 1: Action required
For emails that need you to complete a task or follow-up.

Add these tasks to your Urgency vs Importance Matrix in the appropriate box and visit this folder at a set time every week to archive emails containing tasks that have been completed.

Folder 2: Awaiting response
For emails you expect important responses to, maybe from a client, a team member or your boss.

Again, visit this folder every week. Did you get the response? Does that response mean there's now an action required? Does the email string now need to move to the action required folder?

Folder 3: Delegated

For emails you've delegated to others.

Use your Delegation worksheet to keep a track of what has been delegated and to who, and when the task needs to be completed.

Folder 4: Archived

For emails you want out of your inbox without deleting them completely.

If you want to get your inbox to zero

- Delete – ask 'Is this relevant to me?' 'Am I just cc'd?' 'Is it something in the four folders that I can now get rid of?'
- Do – ask 'Can I deal with this in two minutes?' If so, do it, do it now and don't put it off.
- Defer – ask 'Will it take longer than two minutes?' 'If so, which of the four folders does it belong in?'

How to manage your relationship with your boss

Back in Chapter 2 we talked about team dynamics, and how we all work in different ways; we communicate in different ways, we want to receive communication in different forms, and we get pleasure out of doing different tasks. Well, just as you need to know your team well in order to manage them, you need to know your boss well in order to build an effective and enjoyable working relationship. Who they are, what makes them tick, what they love and what they hate should be very important to you.

- Are they visual, or do they prefer spreadsheets?
- Do they want the whole story or just the facts?
- Are they big picture, or do they want every detail?

If they've done their Team Contribution profile, then you'll have a clear understanding of what they need from you and how best to communicate with them. If they haven't, simply give them what they need in the way that they need it, before they need it. Easy!

Tips for a great working relationship with your boss

Get the basics right

Sounds like a no-brainer but be the manager that your boss can rely on to get the basics right. Be the consistent person who shows up on time, works effectively, completes their work to a high standard and, of course, meets deadlines. This is possibly what got you the manager gig in the first place, so it should be a no-brainer for you.

Understand their goals

Get very clear about what your boss is looking to achieve and what their priorities are. If you've worked with them to set your 90-day goals, this should already be clear. Make sure that you're on the same page, and that you, your boss and your team, are all pulling in the same direction.

Communicate regularly and effectively

It's so important that you understand how your boss wants to be communicated with and how regularly they want to receive reports and updates. Even if you see each other every day, make sure that you agree a time each week where you sit down and have a formal meeting, just as you would with your team.

Don't be afraid to challenge

There will be times, perhaps lots of them, when your boss flies in with a new idea or a new priority for you, insisting that it's urgent. Don't be afraid to challenge them by saying, 'That sounds like a great idea, and of course I'm happy to work on it, but I'm currently working on this, this and this as a priority – which of these would you like me to delay/drop/ put on hold, to make room for this new task?'

In this way, you are remaining positive, but also asking your boss to determine the real priority, and what you'll often find is that they decide that their new idea can wait a while. When this happens, make a note of it, so that you can bring it up in one of your catch-up meetings further down the line, to show that you haven't forgotten it.

Be the manager you would want to work with

If you were in your boss's position what would you want? Someone who brings you solutions to problems, not just problems. Someone who anticipates what will be needed and acts quickly. Someone who keeps challenges with the team away from you, and keeps the team engaged, positive and productive. Someone who delivers results. Someone who is always honest and tells it like it is, even when it's not what you want to hear. Someone who has your back and is loyal to you and the business. Be that manager.

Build the relationship

Remember that your boss is a human being who will make mistakes, have off-days and do things that make you mad as hell. When these things happen, take a breath. Just as you would with your team, when you notice they're stressed or frustrated, talk to them, show an interest, show that you care about them as a person. Be friendly, but not best friends – maintaining that little bit of distance shows respect for their position and gives them room to make the difficult decisions when they need to. Be kind and focus on building a trusted relationship that you'll both benefit from.

Know your numbers

To be a real asset to the business, you need to understand both the big picture and the key numbers that make the business tick.

At the very least, you need to know the key performance indicators (the most important measures of performance) for your business, but you will add even greater value when you also understand and manage the following:

- The critical performance measures for your team that you must stay on top of.
- Your team targets, and your performance against them.

- Your team's contribution to business revenue as a whole and per person.
- Your team spend – on travel, on photocopying, on office supplies. Are expenses going up or are they under control?
- Ways to simplify and streamline your team's operation.

Your boss will be demanding of you, of that there's no doubt – they've given you the new role and the new salary to go with it, and their expectations will be high. How you manage those expectations, while protecting your own time, and developing the team, will be crucial to their perception of your success as a manager.

Your time and energy are very precious. It's vital that you protect and manage both. Put your own oxygen mask on first – develop an effective personal management system and then master it.

Your mission

Go back through this chapter and think about where most of your time is lost. Is your biggest time vampire your inbox, or is it one of the other usual suspects – your team, your boss, or your own inability to prioritise? Uncover your biggest culprit and then focus on taking simple steps every day to control it. Set this as one of your personal 90-day goals, and by the end of that timeframe, you will have developed lasting habits that will keep it under control, permanently.

Epilogue:

Mission complete?

Not likely! Leaders are always learning.

Successful leader-managers understand the need to keep learning and to find learning opportunities in a wide variety of places – through books, through learning new skills, through self-study, through work-sponsored programmes. They learn from their employees, their peers, their boss, and may even find themselves a mentor.

Successful leader-managers all share a passion for continuous improvement and continuous learning – for new skills and new ideas.

Successful leader-managers understand that learning isn't just about business skills. A good manager will network with other managers, face-to-face and online. They'll listen to what's going on in the business world and look for new ideas in other industries, new technologies and new ways of working that they could try out or adopt with their team, for the benefit of the business. They'll listen to their customers, monitor social media channels and learn through their day-to-day communication.

When you take your personal development seriously, when you champion the idea of self-improvement, growth and learning, then your team will see you doing this and are more likely to take their own growth and personal development seriously. They'll become more motivated, more educated and both you and they will find more ways to improve your business and contribute to its growth.

So, what are you going to do next?

- Take time to think about what you learned about yourself as you worked through *Mission: To Manage*. What are you already really good at, what have you become better at as you implemented your new skills and strategies, and what do you recognise as the areas that need more work and more focus?
- Check out the Recommended reading list and the Resources pages for those worksheets and templates we've talked about through the book.
- Consider joining our Managers' Development Programme, which will give you six video training modules, along with the opportunity to get direct access to mentoring and support from me for six months. (More info on page 169.)
- Set a time to meet with your boss to talk through what you've learned, and where you feel you need support.

Resources

Alist of downloadable worksheets and templates by chapter.

Register your book at missiontomanage.co.uk/registermy-book to access your worksheets and templates.

Chapter 1

- Values worksheet

Chapter 2

- A purpose-driven Job Ad example
- A purpose-driven Job Ad template
- Job Description example
- Link to Team Contribution Compass
- Potential vs Performance Matrix

Chapter 3

- How to create a How To (document)
- How to create a How To (video link)
- Link to 1RW Team Tracker
- Delegation worksheet

Chapter 4

- One-Page Performance Review

Chapter 6

- Meeting Plan template
- Meeting Plan example
- Agreements and Actions template
- Our Routines worksheet

Chapter 7

- Urgency vs Importance Matrix

Managers' Development Programme

What it is

The Managers' Development Programme is a structured online programme aimed at developing your mindset and skillset as a manager, giving you the tools you need to build and lead a consistently high performing team.

Over six months you will have access to six video training modules which deal with the basics of people management that you've learned in this book.

Crucially, you will also have the opportunity to join monthly online mentoring and accountability calls where you can discuss specific challenges you are facing, ask questions about the content of the video you've just watched, and share your wins and learns.

On a day-to-day basis, you'll have access to ongoing support from me, my team and your peers through the *Mission: To Manage* private Facebook group.

How you'll benefit

Unlike the usual short courses of a day or a week, the six months of the Managers' Development Programme give you the opportunity to try things out, to make mistakes, and to learn through the feedback you receive from my team and your fellow managers on the mentoring and accountability calls. All of which is crucial, not only in helping you to build your skills as a leader-manager, but also in building your confidence.

> *On a personal level, I've gained confidence, I've become more direct and clear with my expectations. I feel like a manager now, and I can also manage upwards to my boss effectively.*
> Ryn Moser – chief language officer, Supertext

> *I'm only two modules in, but I've already grown in confidence in leading my team and I'm no longer nervous around giving them constructive feedback. Thank you to Marianne for her wisdom and expertise!*
> Maddy Kelly – team manager, Boda Skins

> *Under Marianne's coaching my managers have grown out of all recognition.*
> Jeff Lermer – MD, JLA Chartered Accountants

Where to learn more and sign up

Sound like this could be a perfect way to build on what you've learned in *Mission: To Manage*?

Go to www.missiontomanage.co.uk to learn more and sign up.

Recommended reading

As part of your ongoing personal development, I've pulled together a few of the books on management that I have learned a lot from over the years. I hope you get at least one nugget from each of them to build on what you have learned in *Mission: To Manage*, and to help you in your journey of continuous improvement as a people manager.

The New One Minute Manager by Ken Blanchard
> This easily read story quickly demonstrates three very practical management techniques: One Minute Goals, One Minute Praisings and One Minute Reprimands. The book is brief, the language is simple, and best of all... it works.

The One Minute Manager Meets the Monkey by Ken Blanchard
> This book explains in simple terms how managers can get rid of 'monkeys' – other people's responsibilities – that cling to them and prevent them from managing efficiently. 'There is a high correlation between self-reliance and morale,' says the author, who describes with humour and logic the delicate business of assigning monkeys to the right masters and keeping them healthy. If monkeys are managed properly, you don't have to manage people so much.

The 7 Habits of Highly Effective People by Stephen R. Covey
In this book, Stephen Covey presents a strategy
for solving personal and professional problems.
With penetrating insights and pointed anec-
dotes, Covey reveals a step-by-step pathway
for living with fairness, integrity and human
dignity – principles that give us the security to
adapt to change, and the wisdom and power to
take advantage of the opportunities that change
creates.

The ONE Thing by Gary Keller
In *The ONE Thing*, you'll learn to cut through
the clutter, achieve better results in less time,
build momentum toward your goal, minimise
stress, revive your energy, stay on track and
master what matters to you. *The ONE Thing*
is a New York Times bestseller that delivers
extraordinary results in every area of your life
– work, personal, family and spiritual – and
asks 'what's your ONE thing?'

Eat That Frog! by Brian Tracy
There just isn't enough time for everything
on our to-do list – and there never will be.
Successful people don't try to do everything.
They learn to focus on the most important
tasks and make sure that they get done.

There's an old saying that if the first thing
you do each morning is to eat a live frog,

you'll have the satisfaction of knowing that it's probably the worst thing you'll do all day. Using 'eat that frog' as a metaphor for tackling the most challenging task of your day – the one you are most likely to procrastinate on, but also probably the one that can have the greatest positive impact on your life – *Eat That Frog!* shows you how to zero in on these critical tasks and organise your day. You'll not only get more done faster, but you'll get the right things done.

Leading by Alex Ferguson

This book offers lessons in leadership from the legendary Manchester United manager.

Leading is about leadership, management and the pursuit of success. It looks at leadership from a purely practical perspective, using the raw material of Ferguson's vast experience. If there's one word that characterises his philosophy of management it's *discipline*, and yet what comes through very strongly is humility, and even vulnerability as you realise that his every success has been hard-won. Failure has been a constant threat. Nagging anxiety he just accepted 'as part of my job.' And he wouldn't have had it any other way.

For anyone interested in the subject of leadership, be it managing people effectively and getting the best out of them or learning which qualities and traits separate those who manage and those who inspire, *Leading* is a worthwhile read.